CONTENTS

1) Introduction	1
2) Introduction to The Aspern Papers	15
3) Brief Summary	18
4) Textual Analysis	
Chapter I	20
Chapter II	28
Chapter III	34
Chapter IV	40
Chapter V	46
Chapter VI	53
Chapter VII	58
Chapter VIII	63
Chapter IX	68
5) Character Analyses	72
6) Critical Commentary	75
7) Essay Questions and Answers	77
8) Selected Bibliography	82

BRIGHT NOTES

THE ASPERN PAPERS BY HENRY JAMES

Intelligent Education

Nashville, Tennessee

BRIGHT NOTES: The Aspern Papers
www.BrightNotes.com

No part of this publication may be used or reproduced in any manner whatsoever without written permission, except in the case of brief quotations in critical articles and reviews. For permissions, contact Influence Publishers http://www.influencepublishers.com.

ISBN: 978-1-645421-94-8 (Paperback)
ISBN: 978-1-645421-95-5 (eBook)

Published in accordance with the U.S. Copyright Office Orphan Works and Mass Digitization report of the register of copyrights, June 2015.

Originally published by Monarch Press.
Jane Wexford, 1966
2020 Edition published by Influence Publishers.

Interior design by Lapiz Digital Services. Cover Design by Thinkpen Designs.

Printed in the United States of America.

Library of Congress Cataloging-in-Publication Data forthcoming.
Names: Intelligent Education
Title: BRIGHT NOTES: The Aspern Papers
Subject: STU004000 STUDY AIDS / Book Notes

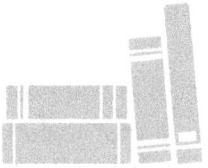

INTRODUCTION

BIOGRAPHY

Henry James was America's first great international novelist. While others before him (Hawthorne, Melville) had written remarkable fiction, they had not left their impress on the universal form of the novel. As Leon Edel, the famous James critic, remarks: "There are few novelists writing today who have not, directly or indirectly, absorbed some of James's methods of story telling." Henry James devoted his adult life to the exploration and understanding of the art of fiction. He conscientiously sought new forms, new modes of expression, new methods of setting down sensation and experience. We are accustomed to thinking of great writers in terms of fascinating adventurous biographies—Byron, Yeats, Lorca, Goethe —but James' private history is singularly undramatic and unremarkable. His great adventures were cerebral.

CHILDHOOD:

James was born on April 15, 1843, in Washington Place, New York City. His father, Henry Sr., had been left independently wealthy by the death of his merchant father. Secure of his fortunes, Henry Sr. had devoted his life to the study of religion, philosophy and humanity. He firmly believed that his children's education should include a thorough, firsthand understanding of their European heritage (grandfather William had arrived in America from Ireland at the end of the 18th century). He acted on this theory with great promptness. When Henry Jr. was in his first year, and his older brother William still a toddler, the family journeyed to France and England. On their return to America, Henry and William received their early education in New York and Albany. In 1855, when Henry was 12, the family once again crossed the ocean. For three years the children were educated by a tutor, by their father and in schools in Geneva, London and Paris. During 1858-59 the family stayed in the fashionable resort of Newport, Rhode Island, where Henry and William studied painting with the well-known artist John LaFarge. But in 1859-60 they were back in Europe again, this time in Bonn and Geneva. By now, at the age of 17, Henry was discovering his great passion for books and writing. In 1862, he enrolled for a brief time in the Law School at Harvard. The same year he sustained a mysterious injury in a fire which kept him out of the Civil War.

LITERARY BEGINNINGS:

Living with his family in Cambridge, James began to meet the important literary minds of the time. Charles Eliot Norton, James Russell Lowell and William Dean Howells were all visitors to the James' drawing room. Exposed to such great stimulation, young James, at 20, resolved to commit his life to writing. This was not the commitment of an idealistic, eccentric young romantic, but rather the mature resolve of a thoughtful intellectual.

James began his public career with a review in the prestigious *North American Review* in 1864, and a story in *The Atlantic Monthly* in 1865. But his first book, a collection of tales, wasn't published until ten years later.

Henry Sr.'s theory of education-by-travel made a great impression on his son. Between 1869 and 1875, Henry Jr. made three trips to the continent. He apprenticed himself to an impressive list of writers in Paris and London: Turgenev, Flaubert, Zola, Ruskin, Tennyson and Browning were among his friends. He knew George Eliot, Renan, Gladstone. James learned his craft in the company of experts.

EXPATRIATE:

An avid traveler, James explored Italy, Germany and France and more and more he discovered that he felt at home in Europe. In 1876, he established himself permanently in London and he continued to live there and in Sussex for the rest of his life.

In 1904, when he returned to America after a twenty-one-year absence, James had mellowed in his harsh opinion of his native land. He agreed to revise and edit his major fiction for a New York publisher and although he returned to England, he made his next trip to America within six years, bringing home his dying brother, William, now a famed philosopher and psychologist.

James was back in England when war broke out in 1914 and with shock and horror he witnessed the holocaust. Outraged at America's refusal to enter the war, James became a British citizen in 1915. The next year he grew weak and ill, and on his deathbed he, was awarded England's Order of Merit. By February of 1916, James was dead.

UNEMBROILED LIFE:

The outward architecture of a man's life sometimes reveals a great deal about his inner existence. Such was not the case with James. His life was devoid of dramatic climactic moments although his literary achievement altered the course of English literature. James had many friends and crowds of acquaintances, but he never married. Among his many friends were a great number of exciting and interesting women, but no letters or gossip give any indication of romantic liaisons. From surviving momenti and from his autobiography, it is clear that James remained, throughout his life, deeply involved with his family. He traveled extensively, he read voluminously, and he labored incessantly at his writing desk. His devotion to his self-designated task at the age of 20 remained constant until his death. And yet, beneath this undramatic architecture lay a mind in continual turmoil and adventure. Behind the almost religious commitment to literature lay doubts, fears, confusion and genius.

PROBLEMS OF SUCCESS:

Public appreciation was elusive and unpredictable throughout James' career. His early writings—tales, essays, travel accounts—appeared with great frequency in important journals, but they gained little following for the young writer. Then, in 1879, with the publication of *Daisy Miller* and again in 1881, with *Portrait of a Lady*, James became an international celebrity. But rapid fame was followed by public disinterest and disfavor. As his works became more complicated, the writer became less understood: his following dwindled. Always sensitive to the reality that a novel must be read in order to be important or influential, James frequently became disheartened at the size of his audience. Although he always had a devout core of eager readers, generally intellectuals appreciative of his master craftsmanship, when the public rejected him, James became despondent. He moaned that he was "condemned apparently to eternal silence," that his finest work "reduced the desire, and the demand, of [his] productions to zero." When the sumptuous New York Edition came out (1907-1917) James called it a "complete failure" and he complained that he was left "high and dry—at my age ... and after my long career, utterly, insurmountably, unsaleable."

The rejection of the artist by society occupied James in many of his stories and tales, and he explored minutely the role of the creative mind struggling in the non-creative world.

James' battle for popular success goes on even today. His modern following is huge and devout—summed up in the English critic F. R. Leavis' words: "What achievement in the art of fiction—fiction as a completely serious art addressed to the adult mind—can we point to in English as surpassing his?" And yet his detractors are still legion. He is accused of failing to come to terms with life, of producing tales of nothingness, and, most damagingly, as Van Wyck Brooks has said, of "magnificent pretensions, petty performances!—the fruits of an irresponsible imagination, of a deranged sense of values, of a mind working in the void, uncorrected by any clear consciousness of human cause and effect."

James, particularly in his later works, is an extremely difficult writer. He insisted that a work composed with care should be read with care—and it takes great care indeed, and very close reading, to reap the rewards of a James work. The reward, however, is well worth the labor.

STYLISTIC PERIODS:

As Leon Edel points out, it is impossible to speak of "a Henry James novel" in the same sense that one speaks of a "Dickens novel" or a "Mark Twain novel." James was continually growing and developing throughout his life and at different phases of his creativity he worked on very different stylistic and theoretical problems. Modern James criticism generally divides his body of works into the following reasonably distinct periods:

1. 1870's: In his late 20's and 30's, James was already a prolific writer. He turned out numerous reviews and articles for the leading periodicals of the day. At the same time he produced major works of fiction: *The American* (1877); *Daisy Miller* (1879); *The Europeans* (1878). In these early years, James was yet a traditional novelist. His characters were straightforward and clearly drawn, lacking the ambiguity and complexity of later heroes. His style was still in the making. Because of their relative simplicity and the themes they explored, *The Portrait of a Lady* (1881) and *Washington Square* (1881) are usually grouped with these early works.

2. 1880's: During these years, James turned his attention to the larger issues in the social world surrounding him. He began to experiment with the involuted style and complicated sentences. *The Princess Casamassima* (1885); *The Bostonians* (1886); *The Tragic Muse* (1887) are the major works of this period. *The Aspern Papers*

(1887) belongs to this period by chronology and style. Thematically, however, it belongs to the next decade.

3. 1890's-THEATRE: During this decade, James turned his hand, with disastrous results, to dramatic writing. Much that he wrote went unproduced, and what productions there were, were miserably received. In 1895, at a production of *Guy Domville*, James was humiliatingly jeered at the final curtain.

4. 1890's-FICTION: These were the years in which James explored in probing detail the qualities of evil and the corruption of innocence. As noted, *The Aspern Papers* belongs, thematically, to this decade. Chronologically, the increasingly complicated works of the period are: *The Spoils of Poynton (1897)*; *What Maisie Knew* (1897); *The Turn of the Screw (1898)*; *The Awkward Age* (1899).

5. 1900's: Ever since the critic F. O. Matthiessen labeled it, this has been known as James' "major phase." Within a few years he published *The Sacred Fount* (1901); *The Wings of the Dove* (1902); *The Ambassadors* (1903); *The Beast in the Jungle* (1903); *The Golden Bowl* (1904); *The American Scene* (1905). His burst of creative energy at this time is awesome. The novels of this period are complex, massive and difficult. They are considered by some to be the best of James, the works of his accomplished maturity. In addition to these major fictions, in 1907, James began the prodigious task of editing and prefacing his own works for a New York publisher. Each preface is an essay on the novel, on the problems of writing, and on the origins of the work under question. The prefaces are masterful studies on the art of fiction, even when considered apart from the works they preface.

6. FINAL PHASE: In the last years of his life, James turned his attention to himself in autobiography. In 1913, he published *A Small Boy and Others,* in 1914, *Notes of a Son and Brother,* and at his death he was working on *The Middle Years.* Also unfinished were two large novels: *The Ivory Tower* and *The Sense of the Past.*

STYLE

Because of his endless tinkering with technique and his continual experimentation with style, James won and lost audiences at a dizzying rate. He was addicted to changes of subject and mood and to variations in method. His problem, and he often expressed it through his stories, was how to turn out an artistically satisfying work while at the same time pleasing the public. His conflict of "potboiler vs. art" was not really much of a contest since art nearly always won out. While his audiences may have been frustrated by his unpredictability, James' experimentation ultimately brought him the reward of true innovation.

The most important innovation, as Leon Edel notes, "was to free the novel, and the short story, of the traditionally ubiquitous and often garrulous narrator who used to interpose his own personality and preachments between the story and the reader."

POINT OF VIEW:

James achieved, in his maturity, the direct involvement of his readers with his characters. He came to call this technique the "point of view," and it was his special method of achieving a thoroughgoing reality. In eradicating himself as omniscent author, James maneuvers us into the consciousness of his characters. We are made to experience events and thoughts directly through the characters and not through the author as interpreter. Thus, in *The Aspern Papers* we only learn of the events as they strike the narrator. We are at all times in his consciousness and we learn only the things he wishes us to know. The problems of this technique are legion. The greatest difficulty is to create a character whose consciousness is interesting enough to sustain us through the novel. If we are to be trapped within one mind for a hundred or more pages, if everything we learn is to be filtered through one awareness, then it had best be a clever awareness. And yet, to maintain his desired level of reality, James cannot present an endless parade of characters of high perception, fluency and literacy—we simply wouldn't believe in them after a while. The critic in *The Aspern Papers* is highly ironic, witty and literate, but he is not altogether sensitive and insightful. The first qualities maintain our interest, the second two help us believe in his reality. Of course the great challenge of this technique, which James met brilliantly in later works, is to sustain our interest in the point of view of a perfectly ordinary, uninspired character. The creation of an average consciousness which fascinates us as it unfolds is James' great genius.

CHARACTER AND PLOT:

A second difficulty in "point of view" comes in simultaneously characterizing and moving the plot forward in the desired direction through that character. Since each man sees the world about him through highly colored, unique and distorted glasses, we must know the construction of those "glasses" in order to judge the true objects on which they focus. If we are to know the characters and follow the events, we must at the same time understand the man who tells us of them, in order to judge what omissions he has made, what coloring he has added and how reliable his descriptions are.

The challenge is as much the reader's as the author's. It is for the reader to put together bits of information he has been given about the main consciousness and then for him to judge how the character would be likely to dissemble and distort. With this information he can then reconstruct the probable objective truth. (When a friend tells us a tale we interpret his narration in light of what we know about his fears, prejudices, anxieties and predispositions—so we must do with James' characters.) The delicacy of the problem lies, of course, in the fact that we must learn both character and plot from the man himself. James' insistence on life-like presentation, forbids the narrator to say: "My name is X, I am Y years old, I have never been married, my ambition supercedes my dignity ... etc." We must learn what we can from the narrator's own natural style. He can never address us directly as readers lest the verisimilitude be shattered and our submersion into his consciousness lost. In *The Aspern Papers* we never learn the critic's age, he is never described to us, and we never even hear his name! We would know these things if he were telling us his tale in person, and this is the effect for which James strives.

NOVEL AS ART:

The development of the "point of view technique" is the visible evidence of James' great effort to raise the novel form to the level of art. Before he applied himself to the form, the novel was used as the author's forum for his own personal philosophy or for social documentation. It was not looked upon as a complete art work in and of itself. James changed that for all time. He forced the examination of the novel's potentials and possibilities. Thus a James novel is not a vehicle for something else. The worlds he creates in his fiction are complete in themselves. James does not seek in his stories to set down some moral law, but rather he attempts, as he put it, to describe the "atmosphere of the mind," to arrive at a satisfactory verbalization of feeling and experience.

INTEGRATED WHOLE:

The structure of a James novel is marked by its unity and germaneness. Ornamentation is never presented for its own sake. Dialogue always moves either plot or characterization forward and description establishes the scene as it is essential to the novel, not as it displays the author's sensibilities. Each scene relates and bears meaning to the whole. The thick texture of James' novels, the richness of allusion, and the ever-increasing density of the created atmosphere render his works complete worlds in themselves. To retell a James plot is to relate very little of the story. Every paragraph depends on the base of sensation and experience built in the preceding paragraphs and every paragraph adds to and enriches that base.

THEMES:

The "Jamesian theme" is one of the favorite topics of critical discussion. Through three decades of prolific output he seemed always to return to a few major conflicts which fascinated him and which he never resolved. James believed in the novelist as historian, as the recorder of the social history, manners and life of his time. In this capacity, he turned over and over the makings of his society (or societies he postulated) and attempted to show his fictionalized characters at one or at odds with their milieu. Contrast and confrontation are the tools James used to explore individuals in their society. A young American girl in Europe *(Daisy Miller, Portrait of a Lady)*, a midwestern man in Europe *(The Ambassadors)*, a man haunted by the image of what he might have been (*The Jolly Corner*), an au courant critic digging into a comfortably hidden past *(The Aspern Papers)*—these are all recognizable James themes.

R. P. Blackmur, the literary critic, divides James' themes into three major categories: the "international theme," the theme of the artist in conflict with society, and the theme of the pilgrim in search of society. These are very broad categories and within them can be contained all the conflicts we associate with James: The Old World vs. The New World; The Past vs. The Present; The Innocent vs. The Corrupt. And these have their own by-themes: the men who fail to understand women; the meddler who is unaware of the consequences of his meddling; the individuals who live by the light of their own egos only to discover they have misinterpreted themselves and others.

Looking at even so short a work as *The Aspern Papers* we can find many of the predominant James themes.

INTERNATIONAL:

The conflict of cultures is constantly brought to the forefront. All three protagonists are on "alien" ground. The Bordereaus have tucked themselves away in a foreign culture they have never fully understood and which surely has never understood them. The critic on his every excursion is struck by the elegance of the dying but formal and historic City and he is somehow at odds with it, until at the final moment, when he deserts his grotesque plan, he perfectly communes with a military statue in an ancient square.

PAST AND PRESENT:

The critic is very much a man of his times, curious and public minded. He has put himself in direct confrontation with a genteel age of privacy. He does not command the weapons of a past age, and attacking with the means of his own day, he meets defeat. The past, however, is not seen as all virtuous. Juliana responds to greed with greed. She is willing to barter with the Present for the Past. Both forces are, to the end, bitterly antagonistic.

INNOCENCE:

Miss Tina embodies this oft-explored James concern. The critic meddles with her innocence and boldly uses her naivete and vulnerability. He is the intruder, the egocentric invader who feels himself and the world in his control. He terribly misjudges the consequences of his meddling and he loses the prize. He also condemns his miserable "innocent" to unforgettable humiliation.

Of all the matters which most occupied James, the clash of the two cultures took predominance. Into it he could incorporate the lesser contrasts. James himself lived in continual conflict between the Old World and the New. He called American life "provincial and uninteresting" and he held that: "It takes an old civilization to set a novelist in motion—a proposition that seems to me so true as to be a truism." And yet, in 1900, during his most prolific years, he told a friend: "If I were to live my life over again I would be an American. I would steep myself in

America ... the mixture of Europe and America which you see in me has proved disastrous."

James summed up his fascination with the "international theme" in terms of the extreme possibilities the subject offered: "[there exists] no possibility of contrast in the human lot so great as that encountered as we turn back and forth between the distinctively American and distinctively European outlook."

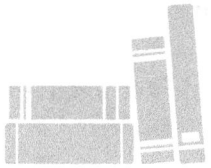

THE ASPERN PAPERS

INTRODUCTION

In one of James' notebooks there is an entry dated "Florence, January 12th, 1887." This entry describes a story James has heard from a friend concerning an American "Shelley-worshipper," a sea captain named Silsbee. The captain had discovered that Jane Clairmont, a long-ago mistress of Byron's, was living in Florence "at a great age" (80 or so) and living with her was a niece of about 50. Silsbee knew that the ladies had interesting letters of Shelley's and Byron's and cherishing the idea of getting hold of them, he schemed to be taken in as a lodger. When the old lady died, Silsbee approached the spinster niece who said: "I will give you all the letters if you marry me!" James' friend told him that Silsbee was running still. The story immediately struck James, and he recorded in his notebook: "Certainly there is a little subject there: the picture of the two faded, queer, poor and discredited old English women - living on into a strange generation, in their musty corner of a foreign town - with those illustrious letters their most precious possession."

The other subject, that of the Shelley fanatic, also intrigued him: "The interest would be in some price that the man has to pay...his hesitations - his struggle - for he really would give almost anything."

In the same notebook entry, James records with alarm that a Countess of his acquaintance had burned a compromising letter of Byron's written to her husband's aunt. (Thus the "gem" for Tina's bonfire.)

During the summer of 1887, six months after he had heard the anecdote, James wrote *The Aspern Papers*. He submitted the tale to *The Atlantic Monthly* and after some delay it was published in 1888.

Twenty years later, while writing the preface to *The Aspern Papers* for the New York Edition, James elaborated on his feelings about the perfect little tale. He marveled that had he known sooner of Jane Clairmont's existence he might himself have looked her up and at any rate he had, unknowingly, frequently passed her very door. The wonder of the "overlap" of the ages, of distant generations touching through an ancient surviving link, overwhelmed him. James, so he said, delighted in the "palpable imaginable visitable past." To be able to reach out and touch through a continuous expanse, the fading past, had for James the fragrance and thrill of poetry. And through his narrator he conveys the wonder of that experience. James explains in his preface the peculiar changes he made from the facts of the original anecdote. He transformed Aspern-Byron into an American as an "experiment." He was curious to see if his own special feeling about the European Byronic age (the reachable past for him) could carry across the sea. "To see in short whether association would carry so far and what the young century might pass for on that side of the modern world where it was not only itself so irremediably youngest, but was bound up with youth in everything else."

James wondered if "a recognizable reflexion of the Byronic age... [could] be picked up on the banks of the Hudson." Since he had transposed Juliana, (for the sake of discretion and disguise), James felt it would be an amusing experiment to "fit her out with an immortalizing poet as transformed as herself."

In answer to the charge that he had foisted "upon our early American annals a distinguished presence for which they yield me absolutely no warrant," James could only say: "I find his link with reality, then, just in the tone of the picture wrought round him." James was not concerned with fitting his characters into an outside reality, but rather in creating a believable world around his characters. His response to the charge of Aspern's "implausibility" reflects his lack of concern with factual credibility. "If through our [American] lean prime Western period no dim and charming ghost of an adventurous lyric genius might by a stretch of fancy flit, if the time was really too hard to 'take' in the light form proposed, the elegant reflexion, then so much the worse for the time...!"

THE ASPERN PAPERS

BRIEF SUMMARY

The richness of *The Aspern Papers* lies not in an action-packed story but in the method of narration and the careful characterization. The plot per se is brief and simple. An American critic (the tale's first person narrator) has spent much of his life collecting material about a famous American poet of the early 19th century, named Jeffrey Aspern. Along with an English colleague, John Cumnor, he has followed Aspern's every step in both Europe and America. The two scholars have recently discovered that an old mistress of Aspern's, now in her 80's, is living with a middle-aged niece in Venice. Cumnor had written to the ancient lady, Juliana Bordereau, asking if she had preserved any of Aspern's papers and letters. After ignoring several of these requests, Juliana finally wrote saying she had no such papers.

The critics remain unconvinced, and the American (our narrator who remains nameless throughout) travels to Venice to see for himself. Using an assumed name, and on the pretext that he has fallen in love with Juliana's garden, he gains admission to the Bordereau "palace" as a lodger. Juliana, clearly aware of what he is after, charges the critic an exorbitant rent, but for three months both she and her niece Miss Tina avoid him completely.

Fearing he is growing impatient, and anxious that he stay on so his rent can be saved for Miss Tina's future, Juliana begins to grant the lodger occasional interviews. Miss Tina, who becomes slightly more available than her aunt, is vaguely courted by the critic in the hopes that she will prevent Juliana from destroying the papers when she feels she is about to die.

One night, in desperation, when Juliana lies close to death, the critic sneaks into her sitting room and begins to look for the papers' hiding place. Juliana discovers him, and with infinite contempt calls him a "publishing scoundrel." The critic leaves the palace the next day for two weeks of travel and when he returns he learns that Juliana has died but that Miss Tina has saved the treasures from destruction.

There is a condition, however. Miss Tina cannot betray her aunt by giving the letters to a stranger. "If you were a relation it would be different," she claims with insufferable embarrassment. The idea of marrying pathetic old Miss Tina is absurd to the critic and he beats a hasty retreat. Upon thinking it over, however, he half-heartedly convinces himself he can "pay the price" for the treasured relics. He goes to Miss Tina the next day on the verge of accepting her pathetic proposal. But during the night she had taken the great step and had burned the papers one by one. With a last unforgettable look, poor Miss Tina retreats into her sitting room, and the critic returns home to his writing desk.

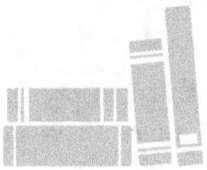

THE ASPERN PAPERS

TEXTUAL ANALYSIS

CHAPTER I

The tale opens with a wonderful, direct statement: "I had taken Mrs. Prest into my confidence." As the chapter progresses, we learn what that confidence is. The narrator, who throughout the story remains nameless, is an American critic and editor at work for many years with an English colleague, John Cumnor, on collecting and editing the papers and works of a long dead literary "god," the poet Jeffrey Aspern. He has recently discovered that one of Aspern's mistresses is still alive at a "venerable age" and is sequestered with a middle-aged niece (or possibly grand-niece) in a dilapidated "palace" in Venice.

John Cumnor had tried to contact the ancient mistress, Miss Juliana Bordereau, by mail, but no notice had been taken of his first letter and his second letter had been answered by the niece in a curt six lines saying that Miss Bordereau had none of Mr. Aspern's "literary remains" and if she had, she "wouldn't have dreamed of showing them to any one on any account whatever."

The editors had been greatly encouraged by this communication because the letter had referred to "Mr. Aspern." It proves familiarity," the narrator tells his friend Mrs. Prest. "You don't say 'Mr.' Shakespeare." They were firmly convinced that Juliana possessed many momenti and papers that would be valuable to the "temple" of Jeffrey Aspern - the temple of which Cumnor and his American colleague were the self-appointed ministers.

Since Cumnor's name and handwriting were now known to the Misses Bordereau, (and even if he assumed a false name, if asked directly his integrity would have insisted that he confess to being the letter writer), it was decided that the American editor, under a "nom de guerre" should attempt to wrest the literary valuables from the ladies by direct confrontation. His problem, now, he confesses to Mrs. Prest, is how to get to see them, no less persuade them to sacrifice their treasures on the altar of the great Jeffrey.

Mrs. Prest, a transplanted American, doing good in the American colony in Venice for the past fifteen years, threw off a "bold conception." "Simply make them take you in on the footing of a lodger." Mrs. Prest, with her thorough knowledge of all Americans in Venice (and the Bordereaus had originally been American although through their long exile and mysterious ways they had somehow lost "all national quality") knew of the ladies, but had only been to see them once many years ago when she had heard that Juliana might be ill. She had not even been invited to sit down by the niece who received her.

All Mrs. Prest knew was that the ladies' name "had been mixed up ages before with one of the greatest names of the century, and they now lived obscurely...on very small means, unvisited, unapproachable in a... dilapidated old palace." Ever helpful, Mrs. Prest offers to row her friend to the palace in her gondola, making no effort to conceal her amusement at his "fine case of monomania." "One would think you expected from it the answer to the riddle of the universe," she goads him. And the narrator confesses: "I denied the impeachment only by replying that if I had to choose between that precious solution and a bundle of Jeffrey Aspern's letters I know indeed which would appear to me the greater boon."

For the narrator, Jeffrey Aspern is a god who "hangs high in the heaven of our literature for all the world to see; he's a part of the light by which we walk." In his day, (the early part of the 19th century), Aspern had been not only one of the most brilliant minds but also "one of the most genial men and one of the handsomest." In their careful studies to date, Cumnor and our critic had found only one "dark spot" in the revered memory of Aspern, and that was his early death - unless, of course, "the papers in Miss Bordereau's hands should perversely bring out others." There had been an impression "about 1825" that Aspern had treated Miss Bordereau somewhat badly (along with some other enamored ladies in England, France, Germany and Italy, where he traveled and wrote in his self-exile from his native America). And if the editors could lay hold of Juliana's papers they could shed more light on the truth of Aspern's life, "the truth, which alone at such a distance of time we could be interested in establishing."

As for Juliana herself, she represents for the narrator a mysterious and incredible link with the divine Jeffrey. The very house in which she lives: "Jeffrey Aspern had never been in it that I knew of, but some note of his voice seemed to abide there by a roundabout implication and in a 'dying fall'"; Juliana's great age, her spanning of the vast gulf of years between Aspern and his adorer, her eyes "into which he had looked," her "hand that his had touched" and most of all her obscurity in this latter half of the 19th century - her ability to have eluded without effort the inexhaustible critics - all fill the scholar with wonder.

When Mrs. Prest's gondola finally stops before the old palace, the critic finds it has "an air not so much of decay as of quiet discouragement, as if it had rather missed its career." Mrs. Prest finds it charming: "It's gray and pink!" But the quiet corner on which it stands she finds "as negative...as a Protestant Sunday."

The critic is discouraged by the size of the place - why should anyone living in such a big house need to take in a lodger. But Mrs. Prest encourages him, explaining that a house like that is "consistent with a state of penury" in Venice. At the same time he is cheered by an overgrown garden attached to one side of the palace - he will use the garden and the sanctity it provides for a writer hard at work as his excuse for wanting lodgings.

At Mrs. Prest's urging, the critic determines to make his first attack on the palace right away. He is well armed: he has had calling cards printed with his false "nom de guerre," he has arranged for his banker to receive his regular mail and for John Cumnor to write him at the Bordereau house in a disguised hand and addressed to his assumed name. He is prepared to "roast all summer" in Venice until his mission is accomplished - and should the ladies suspect he is an emissary from the letter-writing Cumnor, he has devised a plan to parry suspicion. "And what may that be?" queries Mrs. Prest. "I hesitated a moment. 'To make love to the niece.' 'Ah,' cried my friend, 'wait till you see her!'"

Comment

This opening chapter resembles nothing so much as an elaborate battle plan. We are given the antagonists, the issues, details of the battleground, the thorny impasses and the milieu of the attack and parry. James lards this expository chapter with battle terms. The narrator has already been to look at the palace "half a dozen times" but he goes again with Mrs. Prest because it charms him "to hover about the place," and to lay "siege to it with my eyes while I consider my plan of campaign." He wonders at "the old woman's having eluded us" for so long and when he arrives at the palace with Mrs. Prest he hesitates to go in immediately: "I wanted still to think I might get a footing, and was afraid to meet failure, for it would leave me, as I remarked to my companion, without another arrow for my bow." The shrewd critic puts down Mrs. Prest's suggestion that he simply offer money for the papers in battle-like terms: "If I should sound that note first I should certainly spoils the game. I can arrive at my spoils only by putting her off guard." And one way he has chosen to put her off guard is with an engraved "nom de guerre." If she yet suspects and thrusts at him, he is ready with a "parry" - wooing the niece. Through subtle use of symbol and metaphor, James has conveyed the sense of battle. Who are the antagonists?

The narrator, through whose eyes the entire attack is and will be seen, is a self-admitted scoundrel: "Hypocrisy, duplicity are my only chance. I'm sorry for it, but there's no baseness I wouldn't commit for Jeffrey Aspern's sake." But not for a moment does he think his baseness is unwarranted. The world has recognized Jeffrey Aspern as a great genius, the multitude now flocks to his temple, and as ministers of that temple, Cumnor and his colleague are compelled to open as many lights as they can into Aspern's life. As a fully committed critic and editor, our narrator cannot consider the delicacy of Juliana's feelings - the public is entitled to know the full private truth about its heroes.

But the diligent editor, as we glimpse him through his own words and consciousness, is not wholly inhumane. He is ironic and humorous and gently self-critical. He admits that "some people now consider I believe that we have overdone" our probings into the past. He comments, upon hearing Mrs. Prest was not even invited to sit down at the Bordereau house: "This was not encouraging for me who wished to sit so fast."

Although he is a hard-headed fact-getter of modernity, (the modernity of the late 1800's), he is tremendously awed by Juliana's proximity to the glorified past. "The strange thing had been for me to discover in England that she was still alive: it was as if I had been told Mrs. Siddons was, or Queen Caroline, or the famous Lady Hamilton, for it seemed to me that she belonged to a generation as extinct." Juliana is a reachable, touchable link with a past distant enough to be historic, but through her aging eyes and hands and memories not wholly unseeable or unreachable. This is a thrilling prospect for the absorbed critic (and for Henry James who might, if he had known, have thus visited Byron's aged mistress Jane Clairmont).

Juliana, for her part, and all we know of her part thus far is what our narrator has chosen to tell us, Juliana is an antagonist from another age. She reveres privacy above the "public good" - if bright lights cast on its heroes is the public good. "The old woman won't have her relics and tokens so much as spoken of: they're personal, delicate, intimate, and she hasn't the feelings of the day."

The location of the "battle" is itself filled with mystery, romance and contrasts. On one side we see "the bright Venetian picture framed on either side by the moveable window" of a gondola, on the other a tidy corner, "eccentrically neat" and as "negative as a Protestant Sunday." And in this tidy corner, in extreme dilapidation with crumbling plaster, a grey palace all rosy in the April sunset.

James' style is so evocative and suggestive that we are immediately caught up in the awesomeness of the critic's task (as we glimpse it through his own consciousness), while at the same time we are given a more objective perspective through the slightly cynical Mrs. Prest. She has been "tending to" the America colony in Venice for fifteen years, looking in on the ill and hard pressed. She is not particularly impressed by the packet of letters (which she is not convinced even exist) nor is she overwhelmed by Juliana, who after all did have an illicit affair in her youth. Mrs. Prest is clearly an old friend of the critic and eager to help him (as she is eager to help all her fellow Americans abroad) but she is singularly unimpressed with the mystery of Juliana's treasures. Her suggestions: "make them take you in on the footing of a lodger"; why not offer them "a sum of money down" for the letters; "well, perhaps they really haven't anything. If they deny it flat how are you sure?" lend a slightly ridiculous air to the critic's monomania. Mrs. Prest does not wholly approve of the scholar's "invasion" and through her clear-headed statements, which cannot but compel the reader to consider them seriously, James is giving us the hint that we are not meant to approve unequivocally either.

It is interesting to note how James has altered the "facts" of the anecdote as they originally came to him. Jane Clairmont and her niece were Englishwomen living in Florence. Juliana and her grand-niece are Americans transplanted to Venice. The Clairmonts' "god," Byron, was English; Jeffrey Aspern is American. James discusses his liberty with the facts in his preface to the tale (see introduction above) but in fact he takes little pains to disguise the original model. Aspern is clearly an American copy of Byron (as if such were imaginable in America's age of rugged expansion). As with Byron, "half the women of his time...had flung themselves at Aspern's head."

And, as was true with Byron, "accidents, some of them grave, had not failed to occur." Aspern lived, like Byron, during an age in which he had been more than "only one of the most brilliant minds of his day - and in those years, when the century was young, there were, as every one knows, many." Although Byron and Miss Clairmont were his models, the tale is so clearly Henry James' (or, as we come upon it, the narrator's) that it is of only academic importance (of the sort that would delight our narrator-editor) that the characters had a traceable history.

THE ASPERN PAPERS

TEXTUAL ANALYSIS

CHAPTER II

Five minutes after he had floated up to the palace, the prospective lodger found himself in "the long, dusky sala, where the bare scagliola (an imitation of granite or marble, made of finely ground gypsum mixed with glue) floor gleamed vaguely in a chink of the closed shutter." He had arranged with Mrs. Prest to meet in half an hour at a neighboring water-step and had launched his first attack on the palace.

In response to his pull of the "rusty bell-wire," a young maidservant, after much peeking out, had admitted him to the ground floor. The critic had given the girl his false calling card with the message for her mistress in Italian: "Could you very kindly see a gentleman, a traveling American, for a moment?" When she closed the door behind him, the critic "felt my foot in the citadel and promised myself ever so firmly to keep it there." Uninvited, the scholar followed the maid "across the damp stony lower hall" and up the high staircase. The chapter opens as he waits in the gloomy sala for the maid to return from the "impenetrable regions" at the other end of the musty yet nobly shaped passage.

The critic had determined that he should use the weedy, overgrown garden he had glimpsed from the canal as an excuse for seeking lodgings. With this in mind, he moves rapidly toward the lady who eventually emerges from the gloom, exclaiming in Italian: "The garden, the garden - do me the pleasure to tell me if it's yours!" She answers in English: "Nothing here is mine."

The "lady" is Juliana Bordereau's middle-aged grand-niece Miss Tina - "a long lean pale person, habited apparently in a dull-colored dressing-gown." With great eagerness, the critic presses the bewildered niece for details of the garden. "I'm afraid you will think me horribly intrusive, but you know I must have a garden." He explains to her that he intends to be in Venice some weeks and, "having some literary work...to do so that I must be quiet and yet if possible a great deal in the open air," he considers a garden indispensable. Miss Tina does not know what to make of the stranger. Without being asked, he advances toward the closed shutters to get a better view of the garden, all the while extolling the virtues of flowers: "Naturally in a place like Venice gardens are rare. It's absurd if you like, for a man, but I can't live without flowers."

The lady protests that the garden is overgrown and has but a few common flowers in it. To which the scholar replies: "I'll put in a gardener." Baffled, Miss Tina finally gasps: "We don't know you - we don't know you."

The scholar insists "if you're English I'm almost a countryman" and then he feigns great surprise upon learning she is, like himself, American. Through pretence of total ignorance, the intruder maneuvers Miss Tina into telling him that she lives alone with her aged aunt. He finally broaches his goal directly: "Why you surely don't live (two quiet women - I see you are quiet, at any rate) in fifty rooms! Couldn't you for a good rent let me two or three?" With insistent patter about filling the house with flowers and paternalistic chatter about the ladies' lack of economy in keeping so many rooms empty, the critic elicits a promise from Miss Tina that she will "refer the question to her aunt."

And by the way, who is her aunt? "Why Miss Bordereau!" she exclaims "with an air of surprise as if I might have been expected to know." The ladies apparently lived "so that the world shouldn't talk of them or touch them, and yet they had never altogether accepted the idea that it didn't hear of them."

To each of Miss Tina's protests: "the rooms are bare"; "I don't know how you'd sleep, how you'd eat"; the scholar has a soothing solution. He will furnish the rooms, his "man" will cook for him, and anyway: "My tastes and habits are of the simplest; I live on flowers!"

The two part with the understanding that the critic will return the next day for the aunt's decision.

When he rejoins Mrs. Prest, she is skeptical about his hopes of success and chides him for considering the whole thing a wily triumph. Our narrator hastens to assure us: "I did count it as a triumph, but only for the commentator...not for the man, who had not the tradition of personal conquest."

On the return visit, the scholar is conducted by the maid directly upstairs, through the sala and into the apartment from which Miss Tina had emerged the day before. In the "spacious shabby parlour" a strange figure sits alone at one of the windows. And suddenly the critic is "face to face with the Juliana of some of Aspern's most exquisite and most renowned lyrics." He is greatly shaken by being "left alone with so terrible a relic as the aunt," and greatly awed by his nearness to the divine Aspern. On close examination, he sees that Juliana "has over her eyes a horrible green shade which served for her almost as a mask." The critic thinks the shade might have been put on to hide Juliana from view while she could take her visitor in. And then it looks to him like some "ghostly death's head" and finally he realizes how tremendously old she really is, with her small shrunken form bent forward and her head "wrapped in a piece of old black lace." His immediate thoughts are that she will die momentarily and then he corrects that thought: "She would die next week, she would die tomorrow - then I could pounce on her possessions and ransack her drawers."

When Juliana finally speaks, "the remark she made was exactly the most unexpected."

Comment

The great complexity of James' structure and style, his careful juxtaposition of times and tenses, is perfectly exemplified in this chapter's opening paragraphs. The narrator is writing his "history" sometime after the events he describes took place, therefore the whole tale is narrated in the past tense. But it is not a uniform past tense. Without warning, he is likely to talk about the very distant past before he ever came to Venice, or what took place while he was in Venice, or what he and Mrs. Prest discussed weeks after a specific event occurred, or what he learned after he left Venice, and even occasionally what he is thinking at the very moment of writing the tale.

The chapter opens with "I must work the garden - I must work the garden" which sounds like a piece of dialogue we hear at the time it is spoken. But it turns out, we learn a page later, that this is what the narrator was thinking years ago in Venice as he waited to meet Miss Bordereau. We go from this thought to a description of details of event and thought as the narrator leaves Mrs. Prest's gondola and enters the palace. From here we return to him as he waits upstairs in the sala. In between the sequences we may hear of something the narrator is thinking at the moment of narration: "I think [now as I write] that she [the maid] had meant I should wait for her below." Or we may hear of something he is to learn a few months after the time he is generally describing: "There were contradictions...in Miss Tina which, as I observed later, contributed to make her rather pleasingly incalculable and interesting." And for all its being a narration of events as they occur, it is a tale told in the past as a description of a history that happened some indefinite time ago. What is important is that we never leave the narrator's consciousness. As he talks to us, he projects himself, and us with him, back and forth in time so that we are totally involved in him and his experiences.

Supporting the whole of the narrator's structure, is the real author - Henry James. It is he, after all, who wrote the tale and not his narrator, although we never hear from James directly. Everything we learn is from the narrator's own thought and experience. Thus, throughout the tale are woven threads from the narrator's past (not necessarily in any chronological order) and occasionally threads from his present. It is an intricate and thick-textured fabric, and James' great contribution to the art of the novel was the analysis of the fibers of such a fabric and their resynthesis into a flawless whole.

Since everything we hear is from the narrator's point of view, we can't help but learn something about his own character as well as about the events and people he describes. In this second chapter we learn a great deal about him. He has neither a high regard for nor a great deal of success with women: "She [Mrs. Prest] had put the idea into my head and now - so little are women to be counted on - she appeared to take a despondent view of it."; "[I] had not the tradition of personal conquest." He thinks himself pretty clever to have tricked the innocent Miss Tina into thinking he is a passing stranger mad for flowers. And he is delighted with his own astuteness in handling her: "I saw in a moment my good lady had never before been spoken to in any such fashion" - he might as well have added "how deucedly clever I was!" At the same time, we discover how involved the critic is with his task: "as she [Juliana] sat there before me my heart beat as fast as if the miracle of resurrection had taken place for my benefit." And to the extent that he is involved, he is also desperate to succeed even if he has to ransack the drawers of an old woman just dead. The narrator cannot be proud of such thoughts, and while we are grateful for his candidness, we are hardly without reservation when confronted with a man who has them.

THE ASPERN PAPERS

TEXTUAL ANALYSIS

CHAPTER III

The opening remark that Juliana made to the critic, the one that was "exactly the most unexpected" was: "Our house is very far from the centre, but the little canal is very comme il faut." Juliana, sitting hunched by the window with her green eyeshade and lace hair covering, had yet the remnants of her old grace. Her voice was very thin and weak, but "it had an agreeable, cultivated murmur" and after all it was the voice that had sounded in Jeffrey Aspern's ear. Juliana's face (partially hidden by the shade) was now bleached and shriveled but it "had a delicacy which once must have been great. She had been very fair, she had had a wonderful complexion."

In response to Juliana's startling opening, the scholar, after being assigned a chair at some distance from the lady, launched into a rhapsodic tirade about the charms of the palace, apologized for his boldness at daring to intrude without an introduction, and carried on about how much he loved gardens and Juliana's garden in particular. When he was all through, Juliana sat very still and finally said: "If you're so fond of a garden why don't you go to terra firma, where there are so many far better than this?" With what he thought to be an exceptional "flight of fancy," the critic replied: "It's the idea of a garden in the middle of the sea." "This isn't the middle of the sea; you can't so much as see the water." The critic, to our amusement, but not to his, reports: "I stared a moment, wondering if she wished to convict me of fraud."

While on the subject of canals, the critic assured Juliana that his gondola would be at her disposal. Since such an offer at first meeting is in questionable taste, the critic was afraid he might appear "too eager, too possessed of a hidden motive." Juliana's ensuing silence and her impenetrable attitude worried him "by suggesting that she had a fuller vision of me than I had of her."

As conversation resumed, Juliana informed the critic that her niece would be in soon, but she had wanted to see him alone first for reasons of her own. They chat briefly about the niece, then Juliana blurts out: "I don't care who you may be - I don't want to know; it signifies very little today." Feeling himself about to be dismissed, the critic is greatly surprised when Juliana says in a soft quaver: "You may have as many rooms as you like - if you'll pay me a good deal of money." The critic's reaction is delightful:

I hesitated but an instant, long enough to measure what she meant in particular by this condition. First it struck me that she must have really a large sum in her mind; then I reasoned quickly that her idea of a large sum would probably not correspond to my own.

With scarcely any hesitation, the critic assures her he will pay whatever she thinks proper. "Well then, a thousand francs a month," she said instantly. Entire palaces in out of the way corners of Venice rented for that sum by the year! With hardly a murmur, however, the critic agreed to the sum, saying he would give her three months in advance the next day: "If she had asked five times as much I should have risen to the occasion. So odious would it have seemed to me to stand chaffering with Aspern's Juliana."

Just then Miss Tina enters and Juliana cries out almost gaily: "He'll give three thousand - three thousand tomorrow!" The next three lines of dialogue are a classic exchange of comic irony: Miss Tina "Do you mean francs?" Juliana (to the critic) "Did you mean francs or dollars?" The critic (sturdily) "I think francs were what you said." Of course, 1,000 dollars is incredibly more than 1,000 francs.

They make arrangements for the critic to come with the money the next day at noon, and as he rises to leave, he moves to shake hands on the contract feeling "an irresistible desire to hold in my own for a moment the hand Jeffrey Aspern had pressed." Juliana puts him off coldly: "I belong to a time when that was not the custom." Shaking Miss Tina's hand instead, the critic is about to leave when Juliana demands: "Shall you bring the money in gold?" Assuming his protective air, the critic queries: "Aren't you a little afraid, after all, of keeping such a sum as that in the house?" To which she replies: "Whom should I be afraid of if I'm not afraid of you?"

Miss Tina and the scholar are then dismissed and in the sala outside the scholar thanks Miss Tina for perhaps putting in a good word for him. "It was the idea of the money," she tells him. "I told her you'd perhaps pay largely... I told her I thought you were rich."

At the critic's prodding, Miss Tina shows him his quarters on the second floor. There are many rooms, all neglected and dusty. Miss Tina made no apologies for the mess and the critic is disturbed by this: "I said to myself that this was a sing Juliana and her niece - disenchanting idea! - were untidy persons with low Italian standards." While looking around the bare rooms, Miss Tina remarks irrelevantly: "I don't know whether it will make any difference to you, but the money is for me." What money? "The money you're going to bring." Although the critic is irritated that these women associated with Aspern are constantly bringing "the pecuniary question back," he assures her that he is delighted to contribute to her security. "She wants me to have more. She thinks she's going to die," confesses Miss Tina. They discuss Juliana's view of death - she is very tired and would like to die. The critic's thoughts are on the papers she might destroy on her death bed - the papers which he is sure she presses nightly to her withered lips. As they discuss Juliana and her great pride, and the probability that she will remain wholly aloof from her lodger, the critic asks: "Do you suppose she has some suspicion of me?" Miss Tina, giving no sign he had "touched a mark" replies: "I shouldn't think so - letting you in after all so easily." After the critic urges Miss Tina not to remain totally aloof, the lady suddenly departs leaving the strange lodger all alone upstairs. He reflects in his solitude, that "after all this treatment showed confidence."

Comment

From this first encounter, we learn what a formidable opponent Juliana will be. She clearly has the critic's "number" and is in no doubt about his mission. Her method is to lure him - "the little canal is comme il faut" - and then trap him for 1,000 francs a month. The ironic contrast between the critic's romantic view of the Juliana of the poems, and the hard-headed old woman who will milk him dry for her niece's security, is a bitter and comic Jamesian touch. The scholar is irritated by Juliana's talk of money when such vital things as Aspern's papers are at stake - they are above talk of money. But, ironically, he does not feel they are above the deception, hypocrisy and intrusion he must practice to lay his hands on them.

Juliana is so marvelous with her green eyeshade, acid directness and imperiousness that even though we hear the tale from the critic's point of view, we are intended (by James) to be in sympathy with his adversary. Not that we see her without fault. For she, too, is using her lodger, playing on his needs, to her selfish advantage. Although as readers we feel sure that Juliana is on to his game, the narrator himself at this point still thinks himself the clever deceiver. Who but a prying scholar would pay that sum of money for some dusty, bare rooms with or without a garden? Who would take the rooms without seeing them first? Who would bring 3,000 francs in advance without so much as a scrap of paper by way of receipt? Only a man frantic to have entry to a house for ulterior motives - and there can only be one such motive in this house.

But the critic fancies he has taken the ladies in with his chatter about the garden and his familiar paternalistic manner. When Juliana asks for gold, he expresses concern for the wisdom of keeping so much money in the house and then he laughs: "Ah well, I shall be in point of fact a protector and I'll bring gold if you prefer." How self-deceptive we can be if we're blinded by an objective.

Little by little we achieve a sense of the routine and relationship of the two ladies. Juliana notes that Miss Tina "has very good manners; I bred her up myself!" But later the old woman flashes at her niece: "What do you know? You're ignorant." To which Tina replies: "Yes, of money - certainly of money!" Juliana informs the critic, in Tina's presence, that she had tended to her niece's education when she was young "but she [the niece] has learned nothing since." The timid niece replies mildly: "I have always been with you."

When the critic and Miss Tina are alone, she lets him know that the Misses Bordereau will not be concerned with what he is doing and he may do exactly as he likes. The critic perceives she has adopted this tone at Juliana's instruction and he adds: "I may as well say now that I came afterwards to distinguish perfectly (as I believed) between the speeches she made on her own responsibility and those the old woman imposed upon her."

What the old woman had imposed on her was also a sense of her own worthlessness: "She thinks that when I'm alone [after she dies] I shall be a great fool and shan't know how to manage." The critic adds to Juliana's characterization by declaring: "I should have supposed rather that you took care of her. I'm afraid she's very proud."

Miss Tina, (as we see her through the narrator's consciousness), is a timid and sheltered soul riddled by an inward inefficiency. She is a wan and dusty recluse with a childlike innocence and lack of sophistication. She gives the impression of an "irresponsible incompetent youth almost comically at variance with the faded facts of her person."

The characters are becoming more well-defined in this chapter and a slight aura of mystery (the empty, unused rooms, the bare sala, speculations about Juliana's nightly rituals) is permanently established as the new lodger prepares to move in.

THE ASPERN PAPERS

TEXTUAL ANALYSIS

CHAPTER IV

Six weeks later, toward the middle of June, when Mrs. Prest (and her fellow Americans) were preparing to leave the hot city, the scholar had made "no measurable advance." When Mrs. Prest chided him with lacking boldness he had answered: "even to be bold you must have an opportunity: you may push on through a breach, but you can't batter down a dead wall." In his many visits to Mrs. Prest during those six weeks, he had met with chastisement for "wasting precious hours whimpering in her salon" rather than "carrying on the struggle in the field." The narrator with an hilarious bit of unrecognized irony notes: "But I began to feel that it didn't console me to be perpetually chaffed for my scruples, especially since I was really so vigilant." If his vigilance were not a lack of scruple nothing else would ever be one.

Mrs. Prest was, the narrator observes, more disappointed at the lack of drama for her own amusement than at the failure of scholarly advance. "They'll get all your money without showing you a scrap," she goaded him. And so, when Mrs. Prest left for the summer, he settled down to business in earnest.

In all the six weeks the lodger had met his hostesses only once, when he brought "the terrible three thousand francs." At that time, Miss Tina had met him in the hall and with innocent brightness had asked: "Don't you think it's too much?" To which the critic replied that it would "depend on the amount of pleasure I should get for it." In a strange tone Miss Tina had murmured: "Oh pleasure, pleasure - there's no pleasure in this house!" After that the critic had not so much as glimpsed the ladies. They never went out nor did they have visitors. Desperate for some scrap of contact, the invader questioned his servant about their habits. But he could not, or would not, relay any information at all. The lodger had hoped perhaps his servant and Juliana's might become friends or enemies, either alternative being useful for tale-bearing or contact between the employers, but neither happened. Pasquale had his own girl friend who came to visit and he steered clear of the Bordereau maid. The critic concludes: "It was not for me of course to make the domestics tattle." But how he would have welcomed the opportunity to make them do so!

Despite his better judgment, the scholar never asked for a receipt for his 3,000 francs. "If Miss Bordereau suspected me of ulterior aims she would suspect me less if I should be business like and yet I consented not to be." He considered the possibility that Juliana was showing how "she could overreach people who attempted to overreach her." Much later he was to realize that "She had given me part of her house, but she wouldn't add to that so much as a morsel of paper with her name on it."

And yet, the six weeks had not been unpleasant what with endless leisure and the titillating environment. And most of all:

"the sense of playing with my opportunity was much greater after all than any sense of being played with."

To sustain himself, the devoted editor had invoked the spirit of his "god," Aspern. "It was as if his bright ghost had returned to earth to assure me he regarded the affair as his own no less than as mine and that we should see it fraternally and fondly to a conclusion."

The frustrated lodger fed his patience with a sense of communion with the whole world of art. "I felt even a mystic companionship, a moral fraternity with all those who in the past had been the service of art." Meanwhile he lingered around Juliana's door "thinking what treasure probably lurked behind it."

To maintain his pretense, the scholar spent as much time as he could in the garden. He had hired a gardener who, after much toil, had put the place into bloom and the scholar prepared his program of bombardment by nosegay. Before the blooms came, he was in the habit of sitting in a little garden arbor he had set up and over his books he would glance at the closed shutters of Juliana's room (he was sure the ladies peeked out at him although they remained invisible). During those summer days, he fantasied about Jeffrey and Juliana and reconstructed the history he and his colleague Cumnor had put together from Aspern's poems about her. As a young girl, Juliana had come to Europe with her father (a penniless artist) and her sister. Her mother had died when she was young and Juliana "had had in her youth a perverse and reckless, albeit a generous and fascinating character, and she had braved some wondrous chances." The critic mused what her passions had been, for it was clear from Aspern's poems that "there hovered about her name a perfume of impenitent passion, an intimation that she had not been exactly as the respectable young person in general."

THE ASPERN PAPERS

Our narrator had formed as part of his theory the idea that "the young lady had a foreign lover -and say an unedifying tragical rapture - before her meeting with Jeffrey Aspern."

On the other hand, for all this elaborate construction, Cumnor felt sure "that she had been a governess in some family in which the poet visited and that, in consequence of her position, there was from the first something unavowed, or rather something quite clandestine, in their relations." At any rate,

Juliana had been in Europe for seventy-five years and had crossed the ocean at a time when it was a hazardous adventure. Jeffrey had met her there and possibly returned to Europe a second time for her sake but "his own country after all had had most of his life, and his muse...was essentially American." It is the insistent Americanness of Aspern that intrigues the narrator: "When literature was lonely there and art and form almost impossible, he had found means to live and write like one of the first."

Comment

While the chapter starts humorously, with descriptions of Mrs. Prest's remonstrances, it concludes with one of James' most serious concerns - the fate of the creative American in the 19th century and his confrontation with European culture. Aspern had traveled to Europe "before the general transfusion" and his critic "should have liked to see what he could have written without that experience, by which he had incontestably been enriched."

Through the critic, James expresses his search for his own comfortable roots. Aspern's muse, like James', was essentially

American. But Aspern, living "at a period when our native land was nude and crude and provincial, when the famous 'atmosphere' it is supposed to lack was not even missed," Aspern found a means to "be free and general and not at all afraid." James did not, 75 years later than Aspern, find such a means. Not, at any rate in America. Through the critic, he expresses his fascination with an artist who remained true to his American muse.

The critic is spokesman for James only in this passage. Earlier in the chapter he seems more fatuous than scholarly - he shows how truly monomaniacal he is on the subject of Aspern and how blinded he is to the absurdities of his trade. Consider, for instance, this marvelous, unintentional self-parody: "It appeared by some verses addressed to [Juliana] by Aspern on the occasion of his own second absence from America - verses of which Cumnor and I had after infinite conjecture established solidly enough, the date - that she was...as a girl of twenty on the foreign side of the sea. There was a profession in the poem - I hope not just for the phrase - that he had come back for her sake."

Or think of the critic's elaborate, romantic theory about Juliana's father: "It was essential to my hypothesis that this amiable man should have lost his wife, should have been poor and unsuccessful and should have had a second daughter of a disposition quite different from Juliana's." We can just visualize him poring over the lines of verse reconstructing and misconstruing their meaning. And for all his elaboration, his colleague had constructed an entirely different theory based on the premise that Juliana had been a governess!

We not only learn how foolish our narrator can be, we also glimpse the extent of his obsession with Aspern - an obsession that reaches near hallucination. He had conjured up the spirit of Aspern and Aspern seemed to say be patient: "aren't we in Venice together, and what better place is there for the meeting of dear friends?" By his association with Aspern, the critic feels he is working for beauty, for a devotion: "That element was in everything that Jeffrey Aspern had written, and I was only bringing it to light."

The critic, of course, is deceived. He is ignoring the means for the end. Does one devote oneself to beauty by lingering in hallways and watching private doors? By peering over book tops for chinks in the shutters? By pleasurably deceiving a brace of old women? And yet we cannot deny him his genuine fascination with a touchable past - as loathesome as his means to get there may be. The relics he so desperately seeks make his life "continuous, in a fashion, with the illustrious life they had touched at the other end." His goal is not wholly ignoble - his method is.

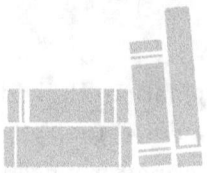

THE ASPERN PAPERS

TEXTUAL ANALYSIS

CHAPTER V

....

The critic passed the hot summer evenings either on the canal in his gondola or in the church square cafes eating ices and chatting with acquaintances. He used to fret about the Misses Bordereau, (with whom he had still made no contact), pent up in their stifling rooms, but "their life seemed miles away from the life of the Piazza."

One evening in the middle of July, the scholar, returning home earlier than usual and seeking the coolness of the garden, came upon Miss Tina seated in one of the bowers. Although he had never suspected she would be there, the critic suddenly felt he had laid a trap for her. As he approached her, Miss Tina blurted out: "Oh dear, I'm so glad you've come," and appeared to be about to throw herself in his arms. "I hasten to add that I escaped the ordeal," the critic comments, "and that she didn't even shake hands with me." Miss Tina was afraid of the dark and the unfamiliar objects of the garden and the critic observes "it was impossible to allow too much for her simplicity."

The scholar questions Miss Tina on her total seclusion and she replies: "Before you came we weren't so private. But I've never been out at night." To the scholar's demand of why he has never been thanked for the armloads of flowers he sends daily, Miss Tina replies: "Why I didn't know they were for me!" And suddenly she asks: "Why in the world do you want so much to know us?" The scholar avoids the question by commenting that the question is her aunt's, not her own. With apparent ease, they chat, sitting on a garden bench for an hour - just as if Miss Tina were an old friend and had not been avoiding him for three months.

They covered much ground that night. And through all of their talk Miss Tina never expressed anxiety about going inside: "It was almost as if she were waiting for something - something I might say to her - and intended to give me my opportunity." Miss Tina told him her aunt had become much weaker in the past few days but she more than ever wished to be alone, and she had almost insisted that Tina go outside and not even stay in her own room alongside Juliana's. The old woman sat still for hours on end and abused Miss Tina when she finally did speak. She ate and drank almost nothing and the great efforts of her day were involved in being dressed and wheeled into the great parlor. Miss Tina chatted on to her sympathetic audience. She described her life in Venice in earlier days. They had had visitors then, at least once a week, and had had occasional sojourns in the town. They had "even been to the Lido in a boat." Most of the old friends had died but a very few old Venetian women and an ancient doctor and lawyer yet survived. These people "came to see them without fail every year."

The critic observes that "poor Miss Tina evidently was of the impression that she had had a dashing youth" when in fact she had had "a glimpse of the Venetian world in its gossiping home-keeping parsimonious professional walks."

Although she was of a generation with the scholar, Miss Tina's reminiscences were so old-world she seemed more Aspern's contemporary than the critic's.

So protected did Miss Tina's life seem, that the scholar felt sure she had never read a line of Aspern's poetry and certainly could not suspect him of being after the poet's papers. As Miss Tina rose at midnight to go, she maintained the chat on a personal level. "Shall you study - shall you read and write-when you go up to your rooms?" And "I shall like the flowers so much better now that I know them also meant for me." The critic felt she was so safe, so plain, mild and innocent he could not resist a "feeler": "In general before I go to sleep... I read some great poet. In nine cases out of ten it's a volume of Jeffrey Aspern." Miss Tina, with perfect seeming innocence, allowed that they had read Aspern, and that her aunt had even known him as a visitor. After expressing great surprise the critic ventures: "Why didn't you tell me before? I should like to ask her about him." Miss Tina says Juliana won't talk about him now. Twenty years ago she still called him a "god" and spoke of how much he had liked her.

The critic, stirred by the opening of the subject, imprudently asks if Juliana has a portrait of Aspern. When he presses the question, Tina replies: "I don't know what she has got. She keeps her things locked up." As Miss Tina mounts the stairs to retire, she suddenly turns and asks: "Do you write about him - do you pry into his life?" After accusing that the question is her aunt's, he suddenly desires to enlist Miss Tina in his ranks: "Yes, I've written about him," he confesses, "and I'm looking for more material. In heaven's name have you got any?" "Santo Dio!" exclaims Miss Tina and hurries out of sight.

For a fortnight after, Miss Tina remained invisible and after four or five days of this treatment, the critic instructed his gardener to stop sending the flowers.

Comment

This fifth chapter is a brilliant example of the viability James can bring to his fictionalized worlds. There is nothing particularly believable about the situation or the characters as we meet them in the garden. But the reality of their relationship, of their complex psychologies, becomes so vivid we don't doubt for a moment the reality of the events.

We can follow throughout the chapter the forces which lead up to the scholar's confession, and although as readers we may not be aware consciously of the deft preparations, they have created an atmosphere which lends verisimilitude to the entire interview and especially to the scholar's confession. It is a lesson in James' style to analyze the atmosphere he carefully creates in that sultry Venetian garden.

Technically, of course, it is the narrator and not James who builds for us. But often he is revealing despite himself, and it is James who has made him so. Several separate strands of atmosphere and relationship inform the chapter and unite in the culminating confession. If we dissect the impressive whole we find first the powerful environment as a force in itself.

The narrator describes the "swarm of noxious insects" that invade his room in the evening heat which is too intense to allow for closed windows. He immediately conveys the restlessness and frustrating irritation that a hot summer's night can bring. The outside world of Venice is filled with beauty, relaxation and companionship but the private world of the Bordereau home, the world he wishes desperately to know, is silent, shuttered, lonely, mysterious and breathless. The garden itself, however, is fragrant, delicious and romantic with "thick flowers"...a reminder that romance (between Juliana and Jeffrey) is at the bottom of his quest. The density of the garden revitalizes his sense of urgency. When Miss Tina finally tells him Juliana thought of Jeffrey as a "god," her tone "stirred [him] deeply as she dropped the words into the summer night; their sound might have been the light rustle of an old unfolded love-letter." Again we hear how strongly this Venetian night matches his purpose.

The last of the interview, conducted in the dim ground floor, is shrouded in protective darkness lit only by a candle. The influence of the night, the garden, the smells, the heat and now partial obscurity in the dimly lit hall all gather and bring forth the confession.

The other strands which ultimately unite are internal. They emerge from the critic's consciousness, from his perceptions, correct or faulty, of Miss Tina.

One of these strands is the critic's perception of himself as potential "lover" - or more correctly, his view of Miss Tina's view of him as potential lover. If she thought of him this way, his secret would be safe with her. Thus, we find sprinkled throughout the chapter references to this implied potential relationship. When he enters the garden, the critic thinks of Romeo and Juliet, of Jeffrey and Juliana and of Miss Tina. But "Miss Tina was not a poet's mistress any more than I was a poet." When he glimpses her shadowy form on a bench, it occurs to him "that some enamoured maidservant had stolen in to keep a tryst with her sweetheart." And as Tina moves toward him, he fancies she moves "almost as if to throw herself in my arms." Although he views the possibility with alarm, a few seconds later he chides her with being "worse off than Carmelite nuns in their cells" without any sort of human contact. The implication is that he would provide relief from celibacy. And to enforce this suggestion he indicates that his feelings have been hurt by her lack of response to his tribute of flowers - the complaint of a spurned suitor.

When the two sit on a garden bench, the critic notes that it is a bench "less secluded, less confidential" than the one in the bower. As if he might be able to compromise the lady on a more private bench!

When Miss Tina rises to go he asks, like a suitor, "when shall I see you again?" When she is vague, he asks her to have faith in him, but he is not persistent for this reason:

I had no wish to have it on my conscience that I might pass for having made love to her. Nothing less should I have seemed to do had I continued to beg a lady to 'believe in me' in an Italian garden on a mid-summer night.

Although he won't ask her to believe in him, he does reply to her artless outburst of "I shall like the flowers better now that I know them also meant for me" with the intimate: "How could you have doubted it? If you'll tell me the kind you like best I'll send a double lot."

The critic has been toying throughout the interview, perhaps subconsciously, with the idea that Miss Tina might view him as a possible suitor and he realizes it won't hurt his purpose to pose as one. It is partially this idea which allows him in the end to be confident that "Miss Tina personally wouldn't in the last resort be less my friend," if he confessed.

The other internal strand weaving throughout the interview is the critic's view of Tina as a pathetic, totally simple, unscheming creature. She has not the facilities for thwarting him and she is so unformed that she is perhaps ripe for his molding. Over and over again, we hear of her meekness: she is afraid of her own garden at night; she has never been out at night; she has led a ridiculously sheltered and uneventful life lacking any excitement or variety; she has adopted the "infantile prattle" of Venetian gossip; she accepts rude abuse from her tyrannical aunt. Innumerable little pieces of information build up the image of the frightened innocent. The critic's narrative is burdened with descriptive words creating the atmosphere of Miss Tina's pathos. She is "simple"; she is a "sad personage"; "poor Miss Tina"; she is "up to nothing at all"; "If she knew little of [the people around her]...she knew still less of anything else"; she is an "innocent"; she is "artless and witless"; she has a "plain mild face." These observations, subtly injected by the narrator, cannot but convince us (as the critic wished himself to be convinced) that Miss Tina could be trusted with anything.

Having played these strains for several pages - the frustrating, provocative summer heat, the confidence of an admired potential suitor, the innocence and simplicity of Miss Tina - we are not wholly surprised when the critic gives in to his impatient temptation, when he decides "Ah yes, she was safe and I could make her safer!" - when he shows his hand despite his careful discipline against doing so.

The preparation has been brilliantly and subtly made - it is a masterpiece of created environment.

THE ASPERN PAPERS

TEXTUAL ANALYSIS

CHAPTER VI

One afternoon in late summer the monotony of the critic's isolation is finally broken. Juliana calls for him: "She wants to talk with you - to know you," Miss Tina informs him. Before he enters Juliana's parlor, he asks the niece whether she has told Juliana of his quest: "If I had told her do you think she'd have sent for you?... I told her nothing," she reassures.

Juliana was sitting in the same place, in the same position and with the same eyeshade as the last interview. Something so grim in the old woman's aspect suddenly struck the scholar that he realized: "as I stood to be measured... I ceased on the spot to doubt her suspecting me...the old woman's brooding instinct had served her."

When he sits before Juliana with Miss Tina at her side, the old woman thanks the critic for his beautiful flowers. She hadn't thanked him while they were coming, but now that they had stopped her propensity for acquisitiveness had risen to the fore and she had summoned him. He immediately offers to renew his tributes that very night.

They speak of the garden and the scholar invites Juliana to come down and enjoy the shade and sweet air. To which she replies: "Oh sir, when I move out of this it won't be to sit in the air, and I'm afraid that any that may be stirring around me, won't be particularly sweet!"

The talk at Juliana's instigation, turns to poetry and then she brings up her lodger's offer of making his gondola available: "Why don't you take the girl out and show her the place?" Despite her niece's protests, Juliana says she shall never miss her at home: "you think you're too important." They arrange that the scholar will take Miss Tina out very soon and as he is about to leave, Juliana asks if these visits are very important to his happiness. "It diverts me more than I can say," he responds. "Don't you know it almost kills me?" she charges.

At the end of the week Miss Tina (who had confided in the scholar that she did not know what had possessed her aunt to behave so differently), Miss Tina consented to an outing in the gondola. She is "transported" by the sights and sounds, and as they head for the piazza she suddenly says: "I've found out what's the matter with my aunt: she's afraid you'll go!... She has had an idea you've not been happy.

That's why she is different now." The scholar establishes that Juliana wants him to stay because of his rent. When he reminds Miss Tina he is anxious to stay for his own reasons, she says: "Why she would never consent to what you want. She has been asked, she has been written to." Suddenly excited, the critic presses: "Then she has papers of value?" "Oh she has everything!" sighs Miss Tina.

Later, as they are having ices on the piazza, the critic questions Miss Tina about her aunt's actions. Miss Tina says that Juliana will probably see him occasionally if that will make him happy enough to stay on. Miss Tina has no idea why Juliana should be so protective of her relics: "It's on account of something - ages ago, before I was born - in her life." But the lady has no suspicion of what that something might be.

The scholar finally broaches his cherished subject. Could Miss Tina prevent Juliana from destroying the papers, which she is likely to do as she approaches death? When Miss Tina says that she cannot control her aunt, the critic muses that even if she doesn't burn them she will have disposed of them in a will, made out, of course, to Miss Tina. "If she has, it's with very strict conditions," she says, implying that she would respect whatever terms there were.

With the evening over, and as they are about to disembark from the gondola, Miss Tina says abruptly: "I'll do what I can to help you." This is some consolation. But in a fretful night hour the critic renews his fears that the old woman is full of craft and might have destroyed the papers that very night in her niece's absence.

Comment

The portrait of Juliana in the opening section of this chapter stands as an excellent portrayal of a cantankerous, unlicensed old woman. By her very aspect (because her glance is invisible behind the shade), she is able to insinuate doubt and accusation. Her words can be cruel and taunting. Her object in this interview, as we learn later from Miss Tina, is to keep her lodger interested in paying the exorbitant rent. She will offer a few enticing tidbits to whet his interest. But from the safety of her age's venerability she cannot resist mocking him. After graciously thanking him for the flowers (indicating she would like him to start sending them again), she taunts him: "What else should you do with them? It isn't a manly taste to make a bower of your room." When he defends his interest in flowers, Juliana throws in: "I suppose you know you can sell them - those you don't use." The scholar replies: "My gardener disposes of them and I ask no questions." Miss Bordereau throws out: "I'd ask a few, I can promise you!" and she laughs an old woman's greedy cackle.

When they speak of the garden, Juliana refers to "that odd thing you've made in the corner" - the "odd thing" is the lodger's carefully planned "summer house." She is capriciously rude because she knows he must and will tolerate any rudeness. Feeling that perhaps he needs a little more encouragement, when the scholar accuses her humorously of being inhuman to him, she taunts:

"In human? That's what the poets used to call the women a hundred years ago." (She will keep him interested by referring to the subject dearest to his heart.)

It is Juliana who proposes that her lodger take Miss Tina in the gondola and show her the sights. When the niece protests she already knows the sights, Juliana cruelly retorts: "Well then go with him and explain... You ought to see them at your age - I don't mean because you're so young - you ought to take chances that come. You're old enough, my dear, and this gentleman won't hurt you."

On taking his leave, the scholar attempts a flattering compliment to Juliana, to which she flashes: "Don't try to pay me a compliment, I've been spoiled." (She reminds him again of her power over him.)

The picture we get of Juliana is of a thoughtless martinet who feels entitled to anything she can get at this advanced age. But she is amusingly direct, so cranky and outrageous in her behavior, that we can only smile at the critic's battle with such a formidable opponent. Miss Tina, unfortunately, is used as a pawn in the battle, and we feel sorry for her; but she is so self-effacing, so incredibly imperceptive, it is hard to give her much thought when her colorful, outspoken aunt holds forth.

The second section of the chapter, the evening's outing, illuminates the first. We hear specifically that Juliana wants her lodger to stay, that she does indeed have those precious papers, and that she has provided for the disposition of her relics in a strictly worded will, that she is capable of having the papers burned before her death, and that she has never told her infantile niece of her compromising relationship with Jeffrey Aspern.

Miss Tina, during the outing, emerges as incredibly stupid and provokingly naive. The only point on which she seems to have any opinion is that upon her aunt's death she will not betray the conditions of the will. Although she offers her services, finally, to do what she can to help, we wonder, as must the critic, what a person so lacking in initiative could ever really do.

This chapter, more than any of the preceding, moves the tale along in terms of action. The papers are coming to the center of focus, Juliana has made herself occasionally available ("My door's shut, but you may sometimes knock"), and Miss Tina has been partially enlisted in the lodger's forces.

THE ASPERN PAPERS

TEXTUAL ANALYSIS

CHAPTER VII

The critic, fearing the papers destroyed, was in a state of panic for several days—days during which he heard nothing from Miss Tina. Able to bear the suspense no longer, he sent his man with a message to the ladies. The servant returned with the news that Juliana had been wheeled into the sala and was looking down at the garden. The critic went to meet her and as he neared she asked: "Have you come to tell me you'll take the rooms for six months more?"

When the lodger protests that the rooms are far too dear for one of his means, she suggests that he can have more for the same price. And, she continues: "If you write books don't you sell them?" Juliana is in a talkative mood and pursues the subject of his career. "What do you write about?" she asks. "About the books of other people," he replies. "What other people?" "Ah better ones than myself... "And what do you say about them?" "I say they sometimes attached themselves to very clever women!"

Juliana refused to react. Her only reply was: "Do you think it's right to rake up the past?"

The critic defends his occupation against Juliana's attacks and suddenly she reverts to her favorite topic: "Well then how much will you give me for six months?" If he had complaints to make "perhaps we can find some way of treating you better." They finally agreed that he will pay by the month, but only twice as much as he would ordinarily pay, not twenty times as much.

As the lodger agonized over whether his negotiations were in vain since Juliana might have burned the papers already, the unpredictable old woman produced from her pocket a small oval portrait. "What would an amateur give me for that?" It was, of course, a miniature of Aspern. The critic feigned ignorance of whose portrait it was, but Juliana would not give him the satisfaction of mentioning Aspern's name.

"He's an old friend of mine, a very distinguished man in his day." They joust in innuendos for a few moments and then Juliana admits : "I know the least I would take, what it occurred to me to ask you about is the most I shall be able to get." The critic reluctantly returns the treasure she had handed him, begging to be kept in mind should Juliana ever decide to sell the portrait.

When Miss Tina comes near, she scolds Juliana for dragging herself about the house. The lodger light-heartedly suggests that next Juliana will pay him a visit upstairs. To which she snaps: "Oh no; I can keep an eye on you from here." She announces that she will see him again tomorrow in the sala. "Shouldn't you perhaps see me better in your sitting room?" he asks solicitously. "Don't you mean shouldn't you have a better chance at me," she returns.

When she is ready to be wheeled back to her room, the critic insists on pushing her. "Oh yes, you may move me this way— you shan't any other!" the old woman cries. Upon reaching Juliana's parlor, Miss Tina dismisses the lodger and takes over the chair. But he cannot resist the temptation to linger a moment and visually ransack the room that harbors the treasures. His eyes are drawn particularly to "a tall old secretary with brass ornaments of the style of the Empire—a receptacle somewhat infirm, but still capable of keeping rare secrets." The avid scholar stares so long at the secretary that Miss Tina notices and changes color. This blush of Tina's convinces him he has located the papers' hiding place.

With great effort he takes leave of Juliana, saying that he will bring her "an opinion about the little picture." Juliana rejoins: "You needn't mind. I've fixed my price." "And what may that be?" "A thousand pounds."

Miss Tina cannot repress an "Oh Lord!" upon hearing this exchange. And when Juliana quickly queries: "Is that what she talks to you about?" the critic leaves his companions saying to Miss Tina: "Imagine your aunt's wanting to know!"

Comment

Comedy on many levels informs this scene in the second floor sala. The thread of narrative which ties together the dialogue and action is highly ironic and mocking. The exchanges between Juliana and the critic are filled with double entendre and innuendo. The silent battle of the miniature portrait borders on slapstick. And pathetic Miss Tina even makes a pun. If we look closely at the comic elements, we see how masterfully James advances the plot, portrays the characters, and at the same time describes an hilarious scene of verbal jousting.

The narrator immediately sets the comic tone when he describes Juliana sitting alone by the window. "The old lady had been wheeled forth into the world and had a certain air, which came mainly perhaps from some brighter element in her dress, of being prepared again to have converse with it. It had not yet, however, begun to flock about her."

Juliana's startling cupidity in her opening question : "Have you come to tell me you'll take the rooms for six months more?" even at this point of the tale has its comic shock value. Through our critic we continue to think of her as gentle Juliana of the odes and we must laugh when she acts like the persistent fish wife. Her lack of delicacy about her niece, although cruel, is highly comic. In response to the scholar's pleasantry about Tina's graciousness in accompanying him to the piazza a few nights before, Juliana snaps: "Well, you brought it on yourself!" But when the "subtle old witch" produces the miniature portrait, the high comedy really begins. Neither of them will mention Aspern's name. And although both of them are sure of the other's knowledge of their own "secret," the charade they have been playing for three months must continue. Juliana calls her most treasured possession one of those "old gimcracks that people pay so much for today." The scholar, who trembles in the presence of the face to which he has devoted his life, exclaims: "What a striking face! Do tell me who it is." Juliana is not to be outdone in coolness. "He's an old friend ... but I'm afraid to mention his name, lest you never should have heard of him." The scholar refuses to take the bait completely and Juliana closes the question with a wry: "It's only a person who should know for himself [who it is] that would give me my price."

When the old woman raises her hand for the picture to be returned, the scholar "instinctively clung to it." A little pantomime ensues, during which the scholar withholds the treasure and the ancient invalid gathers her forces to attack if necessary.

Miss Tina's entrance releases the tension and changes the comic level. Juliana has been asking what Miss Tina talked about on their outing. The critic is reluctant to betray a lady's confidence. "Confidence? Has my niece confidence?" Just then Miss Tina approaches: "Have you confidence, Miss Tina?" the lodger asks. "Not in her, not in her!" declares the dense Tina.

With Miss Tina as witness, the jousting becomes more vigorous, more comic and more direct. "I want to watch you—I want to watch you!" cries Juliana. "Well then let us spend as much of our time together as possible," purrs the lodger. The scholar's visual ransack of Juliana's "faded, unsociable room" is the comic climax of the chapter. He make a great effort to gather up his "slightly scattered prudence" and leave, but not before he had visualized battered boxes shoved under the bed and a "lame dressing table" near the night lamp as possible hiding places. His final choice, the Empire secretary, with its "peevish little lock," presents merely a plain panel as obstacle between him and the goal of his hopes. That panel and lock will soon cause him excruciating embarrassment.

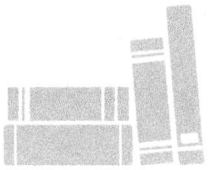

THE ASPERN PAPERS

TEXTUAL ANALYSIS

CHAPTER VIII

....

Three hours after the scholar left Juliana's sitting room, Miss Tina appeared at the doorway of his dining room. "My aunt's, very ill; I think she's dying!" declared the lady. The maid had been sent for a doctor and had not yet returned. Although he suspected Juliana of some weird ruse, the critic sent his own servant after a doctor and accompanied Miss Tina to her aunt's quarters.

Juliana, with the upper part of her face covered by "a piece of dingy lace muslin" was breathing so shallowly as to appear beyond help. Since the old lady was past "human attention" the critic focused on her room, rummaging visually all possible hiding places. Miss Tina again noticed the intensity of his gaze, and taking pity pointed to a trunk under a sofa and said: "Those things were there." "Were there…?" he asked, startled. But the doctor appeared before she had time to answer, and the critic was forced to leave. He waited anxiously in the garden for the doctor to finish and when he finally went in Miss Tina met him in the sala. "She's better, she's better," announces the lady, "there's no immediate danger."

The scholar persuades Miss Tina to wait with him on the balcony of the sala for the doctor's promised return. He promptly raises the question: "And where are they now - the things that were in the trunk?" "In the trunk?" queries Miss Tina. She has had a few other things on her mind. The letters are no longer in the trunk. Miss Tina had searched for them for the scholar. "Do you mean you'd have given them to me if you had found them?" he asks trembling. "I don't know what I'd do - what I wouldn't!" is her confused reply. Miss Tina finds it indecent to explore the subject further while her aunt lies dying: "I can't deceive her - perhaps on her deathbed."

The scholar is abashed enough at Tina's fidelity to her aunt to confess his own deception - that he has been living under a false name. She takes the news good - naturedly, and with that absolution the critic returns to his vital search. "How can she possibly have changed the place herself?" Miss Tina attributes the seemingly impossible effort to Juliana's great will. Despite the lady's attempts to change the subject, the critic persists: "Of course if she can rummage about that way she can perfectly have burnt them." "You must wait - you must wait," moralizes Miss Tina mournfully.

The painful exchange is interrupted by the doctor's arrival and the critic is again left alone with his anxious thoughts. For relief he walks to the piazza, awaiting the proper moment to return for a promised report from Miss Tina on Juliana's condition. When he does return it is after midnight and the sala is dark. When Miss Tina fails to appear, he taps gently on Juliana's sitting room door. There is no answer. Possessed by his desire and discarding all delicacy, he opens the door and enters the darkened sitting room.

In a wild burst of theorizing and rationalization, he makes himself believe that Miss Tina might have unlocked the desk for him and all he need do is push a brass button and the lid will slide open. To test this frantic theory, he bends over to touch the button and on some instinctive whim looks over his shoulder:

Juliana stood there in her nightdress, by the doorway of her room, watching me; her hands were raised, she had lifted the everlasting curtain that covered half her face, and for the first, the last, the only time I beheld her extraordinary eyes. They glared at me; they were like the sudden drench, for a caught burglar, of a flood of gaslight; they made me horribly ashamed. I never shall forget her strange little bent white tottering figure, with its lifted head, her attitude, her expression; neither shall I forget the tone in which as I turned, looking at her, she hissed out passionately, furiously: 'Ah you publishing scoundrel!'

Stammering excuses the critic approaches Juliana. The old lady waves him off in horror and falls back "with a quick spasm" into Miss Tina's arms.

Comment

This climactic chapter focuses on the critic's incredible lack of scruple and decency. He has become so obsessed with his hunt that he has lost the capacity to act like the gentleman he considers himself to be. From the first moment he hears that Juliana is near death, he can only think of his own fortunes and barely considers the hardship for Miss Tina or the horror for

Juliana. His first reaction is to bitterly accuse Juliana of faking her illness to trap him. His second thought, on nearing the death bed, is that now he can get a better look at the object of his study (but Juliana even near death has protected herself from scrutiny).

Finding himself at long last in the secret bedchamber, the scholar avidly turns his attention to possible hiding places in the chaotic room. His curiosity is so direct that Miss Tina can't help noticing it and the poor lady is torn between her dying aunt and her prying lodger.

Again, thinking only of himself, while he waits in the garden he grows impatient with Miss Tina for failing to bring him news - as though she had nothing on her mind other than his success in his parasitic venture. When he is finally alone with Miss Tina, he relentlessly pursues his objectives. Has she looked for him? Will she look again? Must he wait till Juliana dies to find out if she's burned the letters? Must he wait till then to learn if Miss Tina will let him see the treasures? How can the old lady have had the strength to move the bundles? Who helped her do it? The narrator, in retrospect, is ashamed of his insensitivity. But his latter day shame does not lessen the impact of his crude behavior.

The prelude to the climactic discovery by Juliana, the critic's rationalization of his gross invasion, shows how completely he has lost his perspective. He has allowed his slightly absurd pursuit to prevail over any sense of decency or respect.

Returning to the palace late at night, he finds that Miss Tina has left no light for him, no sign that she had waited for his return' He reasons that she has gone to bed. But how could she go to bed with her aunt so ill? When there is no answer to his knock and no light on in the vacant room, he assumes Miss Tina has released him from the promise of a rendezvous. But he is so "anxious" about Juliana he wishes to keep that promised appointment.

Although he makes no noise and does not call Miss Tina, he waits to see if she will emerge from the bedchamber in response to his light tap. She does not, so he reaffirms his assumption that she has fallen asleep. If she is sleeping, her aunt must be better and he can wait 'til tomorrow for news. But the sense of opportunity overcomes the sense of correctness.

He didn't plan thievery, and even if he had, he couldn't smash into the secretary with his bare hands. But perhaps Miss Tina was sleeping so soundly in order to give him "the field." Perhaps she had left the sala door open to provide him opportunity "if she wished me to keep away, why hadn't she locked the door?" Perhaps she had even opened the secretary for him.

Like a possessed man, the scholar creates an unreal world based on deluded premises. His conscience insists on reasons for his gross actions, so he produces them, as fantastic as they are.

Juliana's "discovery scene" is as symbolic as it is dramatic. Her eyes which glare "like the sudden drench, for a caught burglar, of a flood of gaslight" illuminate momentarily for the scholar the shamefulness of his deceptive pursuit. It is as though the furious Juliana has finally brought the bright light to his shady doings and he can no longer hide his selfish motives behind deceits, rationalizations and verbal maneuvers. He is, at the core, a "publishing scoundrel" and even the cloak of dedication to Jeffrey Aspern cannot hide him from this truth hissed out by Juliana at that terrible moment.

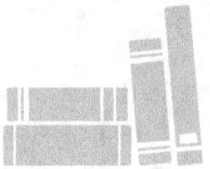

THE ASPERN PAPERS

TEXTUAL ANALYSIS

CHAPTER IX

....

As terrible as that moment of discovery is, the critic rather rapidly restores his defensive equilibrium. Upon learning that Juliana had not died in the night, he departs the next day for a short trip away from Venice. Knowing that the only honorable course would be to leave the Bordereaus alone forever, he nonetheless convinces himself that it wouldn't be fair to Miss Tina to leave so abruptly. Driven by his avarice and consoled by his reason, he returns to Venice after 12 days and learns from his servant that Juliana has died in the interim. He finds Miss Tina in the garden, and to his amazement she is glad to see him. They spend the evening strolling and talking and the critic is solicitous and protective, although he is careful not to imply that he plans to take responsibility for her future. Not a word is said about the Aspern documents as the critic thinks "it more decent not to show greed again so soon after the catastrophe." Miss Tina, for her part, never mentions them.

During the night, the critic imagines no mention was made because the papers are destroyed and he waits eagerly the next day for Miss Tina. He is sure he will learn his quest has ended in destruction and then he will depart immediately: "for seriously... I couldn't linger there to act as guardian to a piece of middle-aged female helplessness."

Miss Tina reassures him that there are "a great many" papers but she can't show them to him. During an incredibly painful, embarrassing interview, Miss Tina finally makes him understand that Juliana had, on her death bed, ordered the papers burned but instead Miss Tina had locked them away. Yet she cannot show them to him. As she died, Juliana "wanted to say something to me...something very particular. But she couldn't." Miss Tina finally lunges: "Well...if you were a relation it would be different...if you weren't a stranger. Then it would be the same for you as for me."

Agonized by this proposal, the critic consults the miniature portrait of Aspern which Miss Tina had presented him moments before. But Aspern's only response is: "Get out of it as you can, my dear fellow!" But he can't. Miss Tina becomes more explicit: "She wanted me to be happy. And if any person should be kind to me... I'd give you everything, and she'd understand, where she is - she'd forgive me!"

The critic can only stammer: "Ah, Miss Tina" before he moves wildly to the door. He spends the day wandering aimlessly about Venice and reconciling himself to the loss of the papers which he and Cumnor can do quite well without anyway. But during the night, fired by the papers' proximity, he swings "back to passionate appreciation of Juliana's treasure." The next morning he goes to Miss Tina. She appears to him now not crushed by his rejection but full of absolution, "angelic; it beautified her; she was younger; she was not a ridiculous old woman." Somewhere from the depths of his conscience comes a whisper: "Why not, after all-why not?"

But Miss Tina in her new "infinite gentleness" with her new "force of soul" has seen him in order to say goodbye: "I've done the great thing," she announces. "I've destroyed the papers." She had burned them one by one and "it took a long time - there were so many." Immediately Tina changes back to a "plain dingy elderly person" and in this form they part.

Sometime later, the critic sent Miss Tina a large sum of money for the miniature portrait of Aspern saying that he had sold it. But in truth it "hangs above my writing-table. When I look at it I can scarcely bear my loss - I mean of the precious papers."

Comment

The bitterly comic proposal sequence has an amazing impact. We really end up caring about poor dusty old Miss Tina and we suffer with her when she puts forth her painful suggestion. James clearly means for us to care. He disapproves of the critic's methods and goals, and Tina's pain is the way he drives home for us the immorality of the critic's invasion.

If there is a lesson to be learned from this tale it lies in Miss Tina's pain. The greedy quest for the private papers (which after all will do much more for him, for his reputation as a critic, than for anyone else) does not go on in a vacuum. If he were digging up old references in a musty library his work might be inconsequential, but not destructive. However, he has chosen to dig up old people, and this form of meddling is tinged with immorality. He knows that Miss Tina has become dangerously dependent on him, and during his twelve-day absence when he debates whether or not to return to the Bordereau house, he decides to disregard the consequences of that dependency. ("Then I reflected that I had better try a short absence first, for I must already have had a sense [unexpressed and dim] that in disappearing completely it wouldn't be merely my own hopes I should condemn to extinction.") We need very little insight to conclude whether it is for his own hopes or Miss Tina's he decides to return.

Yet, for all his lack of consideration we are never fully alienated from our narrator. We know him for a scoundrel, but he tells his tale so artfully and so honestly we cannot wholeheartedly condemn him. His description of his self-deception when he toys with accepting Miss Tina's proposal ("she stood in the middle of the room with a face of mildness bent upon me, and her look of forgiveness, of absolution made her angelic") comes off as an hilarious joke played by his own unconscious. And our narrator is the first to laugh at the joke.

His genuine dedication to Aspern, to Aspern's art, and to the excitement of reachable history attracts our sympathy and prevents us from unequivocally hissing "scoundrel." But his bullish persistence, his urge to test the ladies to their limit, and his ultimate meddling with Miss Tina's untried emotions are unpardonable indiscretions. Our final impression of him, driven home by poor Tina's mortification, is less of a gentleman and a scholar than of a peeping Tom.

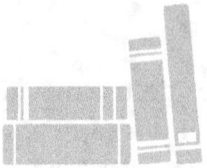

THE ASPERN PAPERS

CHARACTER ANALYSES

THE NARRATOR

Although we are never told his name, age or appearance, we indirectly learn a great deal about our scholar-narrator. He is an American who has travelled widely in Europe. He came from a "good" family and is well educated. He is middle-aged (since he is considered a possible suitor for the middle-aged Miss Tina). He has a fine ironic with which he is frequently able to turn on himself. And yet, he is not altogether likeable. He unscrupulously uses Miss Tina and provokes Juliana to obtain his selfish ends (and they are undoubtedly selfish despite his protestations that he is serving art and humanity). He is so caught up in the petty details of scholarly research that he is no longer able to weigh and judge decent human behavior. He is ready, for instance, to marry the pathetic Miss Tina in order to have at his command somebody else's love letters. The game and victory have become his life's meaning - love, respect, privacy, consideration have all been sacrificed to the game. He is, unquestionably, delightful company. His narration is witty, perceptive, sardonic and fluent - qualities we appreciate as we see the events solely through his consciousness. He is genuinely awed by his connection with the past through Juliana, an awe we can respect and applaud. But he is, for all his wit and intelligence, a scoundrel who will stop at nothing - an exploiter who will excuse all - in order to obtain his ends. He is the blinkered scholar who will head for the facts upsetting all objects and people obstructing the way.

JULIANA

The cantankerous old mistress is a mighty opponent for the critic. She has something he wants, and although she has no intention of giving it to him, she will make him pay through the nose to find that out. Juliana is very vain, very cruel and terribly clever. She plays with the scholar and abuses Miss Tina, taking refuge behind the license of her great age. At the brink of the grave she clings to life greedily and graspingly. She is not above using her sacred relics as blackmail and if they will bring her an income and her niece a provider, then she will shamelessly hold them out as bait.

Because these tactics are employed essentially in defense, (she did not launch the first invasion), we find her more amusing, less reprehensible, than her foe. Juliana is colorful and dangerous. With her withered cheeks, green eyeshade, and acid tongue she is vaguely grotesque but endlessly interesting and unpredictable.

MISS TINA

The dowdy Miss Bordereau is nothing so much as a pawn in the battle between Juliana and her lodger. At the very first meeting with the critic, he senses in her bewilderment and naivete a malleable ally. She has had little converse with the world and whatever companionship he will offer she will gratefully receive.

Except for the brief moment when the critic feels ready to "pay the price," Miss Tina is discussed only in terms of her drabness. She is dusty in appearance and wit. Juliana has only the greatest

disdain for her sheltered, provincial niece, and the lodger, although he uses her shamelessly, views her as a "piece of middle-aged female helplessness." Miss Tina apparently has never had a chance. She has spent her life at the side of her eccentric great-aunt who had long since tasted life's fullest excitements, and Miss Tina never has had a glimpse of gaiety, joy or pleasure. Tina's two final acts - the proposal and the destruction of the papers - are probably the bravest, most stirring moves of her life. She has been pathetically betrayed by the lodger, probably the only person to whom she has ever attempted to reveal herself, and with the destruction of her only drawing card for the outside world, we feel sure she will close herself in Juliana's sitting room and somehow pass the dreary days to death.

MRS. PREST

The sharp, practical, all-knowing expatriate Mrs. Prest serves the role of confidante and objective observer. It is to her the critic turns for advice and it is through her conversations with him that we are given an outsider's view of the events. Mrs. Prest hasn't the foggiest idea who the Misses Bordereau really are - (and neither, we suspect, does the rest of the world). She is not caught up in the vagaries of scholarly research and cannot share the critic's adoration for the ladies or their possessions. She is full of practicality. Make them take you on as a lodger if you want to get into the house. Offer them money outright for the papers instead of waiting to be asked to tea. Mrs. Prest provides objective balance, the viewpoint of the outside world, to the intensity, the intricate ballet of deception being staged in the Bordereau palace.

THE ASPERN PAPERS

CRITICAL COMMENTARY

Perhaps because of its brevity, perhaps because of its perfection, there is little critical controversy concerning *The Aspern Papers*. James' two greatest critics, Leon Edel and F. W. Dupee are in complete agreement as to the tale's merits. Edel calls the story "the most brilliant of all of Henry's tales." Dupee says: "It is first-rate at all points, and so thoroughly realized that it rather defies definition."

Most James scholars, having to choose among the myriad volumes of his work, overlook *The Aspern Papers* because it is not a "major work." However, Dupee in *Henry James: His Life and Writings* discusses the tale. He finds that "the genius of the story is chiefly in the conception of Miss Bordereau herself." Juliana is no "wistful survivor of the past" but rather "a diabolical incarnation of it." She is greedy of her bargaining power with the present, and with her green eyeshade she is more in league with gamblers than gracious old women.

In *The Short Novels of Henry James*, Charles G. Hoffman briefly discusses *The Aspern Papers* as a "significant and convincing portrait of a journalist." He sees the central problem as that "of the artist and his relation to life and to society," and he views the scheming narrator as the corrupter and destroyer of the guileless Tina. The critic, for Hoffman, is the strong center of evil, not Juliana.

Leon Edel, taking a biographical view of the story, sees Juliana as a portrait of a vaguely remembered great aunt of James'. And in *Henry James: the Middle Years,* Edel argues convincingly that the relationship between the critic and Miss Tina is a reflection of and an apologia for James' own relationship at the time he wrote the story with a devoted spinster friend. Edel ties *The Aspern Papers* in with many of James' major themes. It concerns Past and Present, Old and New, corruption of innocence, and the "international theme." With its use of the first person narrator, it foreshadows the "internal monologue" of modern fiction.

Major critical works on Jamesian themes and techniques are applicable in parts to *The Aspern Papers* although rarely is the tale mentioned specifically. There are a bewildering number of critical treatments of James. In those considered by the student, points of interpretation will be easily transferred from the specific work discussed to *The Aspern Papers.*

In the Selected Bibliography below, points of departure for James study are suggested. Further references can be found in the bibliographies of these works.

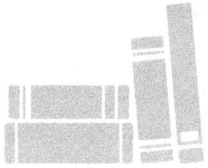

THE ASPERN PAPERS

ESSAY QUESTIONS AND ANSWERS

Question: What are the broad strokes of comedy that inform *The Aspern Papers*?

Answer: Despite its highly moral purpose and its philosophical investigation of relationships with the past, *The Aspern Papers* is basically a comic tale. The major incidents and the confrontations between the characters are informed by a biting comic irony. The very search for the papers, the given of the story, is based on an ironic disparity. The critic is, as he insists, serving high art. He is digging for facts in order to throw light on the "temple" of a great poet. He feels himself at one with the great creative minds of history in that he too is devoting himself to truth and beauty. But in the service of art, in the name of knowledge and truth, he is committing a gross indelicacy and practicing outlandish, if unsuccessful, fraud. His goal may be high-minded, but his methods of reaching that goal are so reprehensible as to invalidate any discoveries he might make. This pretence of seeking the truth while being untruthful, of serving beauty while being gross and insensitive, presents an ironic and highly comic contradiction.

Juliana's ironic disparities are comic to the point of vaudeville. Here is the revered old relic of Aspern's affections, the vital connecting link with a past growing dim, and all she wants to talk about is next month's rent. Juliana never says or does anything lovely, gentle or poetic. She is acid, querulous, cruel and mercenary - in short a caricature of cranky old age. But from this crafty ancient the critic is seeking all the beauty and truth associated with Aspern. Juliana's refusal to fill the role the scholar so longs for her to fill, her insistence on talking cold cash not warm poetry is an hilarious use of the ironic reversal.

Miss Tina, too, is comic, but in a pathetic, puppy dog way. Her stupidity and innocence are banal, her meekness infuriating. And yet this malleable nonentity becomes the insurmountable impasse. With incredible unexpected boldness she offers herself as the price for the papers. The very audacity of the move from the self-effacing spinster makes for high comedy of opposites.

Throughout the tale runs the comic thread of the joust. The lodger does not know if Juliana knows that he knows that she has the papers. And at times, in fact, he does not know if she does have them. The maneuvering, the thrust and parry, tinged with suspense, makes for a marvelous comic battle of words and occasional surprise strategies.

Question: What is the function of John Cumnor in the tale?

Answer: Cumnor, the narrator's fellow scholar-critic, never participates in the relationship established between Juliana, Tina and the narrator. He is only referred to by name. And yet, each time the narrator mentions Cumnor's name he tells us something about himself. Whenever the narrator censors Cumnor, he indirectly censors himself. Cumnor, for instance, ludicrously "confirms" the existence of the Aspern papers on the basis of Juliana's use of the familiar "Mr." in a letter about the poet. Cumnor's absurd hypothesis complements the narrator's equally absurd and elaborate theory about Juliana's past - a biography based on a few scraps of poetic allusion. Cumnor, the narrator tells us, could never have lied to the ladies' faces. If he had come to Venice himself and had been asked by Juliana if he had written the earlier inquiring letter, his sense of honesty would have forced him to confess. This same man, however, can write to the narrator in a disguised handwriting addressing the mail to a false name, in order to deceive the Bordereaus. The narrator's "virtue" has the identical flaw. He extols his own honesty in being able to deny authorship of the earlier letter - he didn't, after all, actually write it. But should the Bordereaus accuse him of being Cumnor's emissary, he would be willing to make love to Miss Tina to parry the blow.

Cumnor is a reflection of the narrator and is used by James to heighten the irony of the disparity between the narrator's words and actions. James uses Cumnor as a device to convey dramatic irony, enabling the narrator to reveal something of his own character without violating the point of view of the story.

Question: How does James use the Bordereau garden for irony and symbol?

Answer: The narrator, ironically, is trapped by his own garden ruse. On the pretense of loving the garden he gains entry to the house. But once in, he must keep face and, at his own expense, cultivate the hopeless mess.

His cultivation of the garden is akin to his cultivation of the house and its inhabitants. In both cases he "attacks" untouched ground, and in both cases he makes perverse use of what he has cultivated. He uses the flowers in the garden as a bribe, as a mercantile exchange for his devious goals. When he is thwarted in his desires, he withholds the flowers. The lodger makes perverse use of nature for unnatural ends. In the same way, he makes perverse use of human relationships. He cultivates the "untouched" Miss Tina for his own selfish ends, and in the holy name of art, love and beauty he wages a highly unscrupulous battle. His misuse of inanimate nature emblemizes his misuse of human nature.

Question: What purpose does the occasional reference to Aspern as a god serve?

Answer: Just as the narrator is willing to pervert nature for his own uses, so both he and Juliana are willing to misuse their "god" for barter and power. The narrator tells us that he and Cumnor consider themselves priests at the altar of Aspern, which had only lately begun to be served by others. He refers to Aspern as a god. Juliana says that Aspern was a god, and Tina tells us that Juliana called the writer of the first letter of inquiry (Cumnor) a devil.

Cumnor and the narrator, if they are priests of a temple, are extremely corrupt and defiling priests. In Aspern's name they sin unpardonably. They use the poet to further their own reputations as critics. Their devotion is false, their cultish worship blind and selfish. Juliana's worship is no more pure. She uses her "god" for financial gain, bartering his very "image" for 1,000 francs.

James is laughing at the cult of critical worship and the sale of literary "relics." There are no literary Gods and those who will set them up are really after a fast dollar or a little bit of second-hand fame.

Question: Why are we able to accept both the horrible and grotesque, the humorous and the understandably human, in the world of James' tale?

Answer: Every masterful stroke with which James tells his story is controlled and purposeful. Each detail contributes to the whole effect of the tale, and in order to fully understand why we accept such disparate elements as one integrated whole, we should pay attention to the way in which each one is handled. The grotesque, for example, is never overdone, so that we reject it from the "realistic" story. Juliana's face is always hidden behind the green eyeshade, behind a veil. The only time she reveals her face is when the narrator invades her room before her death, in search of the papers, revealing his ghoulishness in the light of her eyes which "glared...like the sudden drench...of a flood of gaslight..." It is unusual, it becomes grotesque, for a woman, no matter how old or vain, to hide her face completely until her death. We accept the fact, however, because James handles it so well, never pushing it on us, but rather, using it as an atmospheric touch, subtly underlining the basically inhuman relationships in the villa.

We are able to accept this detail and others like it, along with the humor and the occasional glimpses of warmth, because the world which James has created in *The Aspern Papers* is a given world, it exists on its own terms. The opening of the tale reveals this fact to us. The narrator opens by saying, "I had taken Mrs. Prest into my confidence." Now we, too, are to be taken into his confidence. The universe which is to be revealed to us is something to be confided - is something which exists as it exists and is to be described, not organized and developed before our eyes. It will be presented to us as it exists, not as it grew out of previous relationships and as it might move forward in time.

THE ASPERN PAPERS

SELECTED BIBLIOGRAPHY

BIOGRAPHY

Dupee, F. W., *Henry James* (New York, 1951). This one volume critical biography is an excellent study of James' life and craft. It is a fine starting place for serious or cursory James study.

Edel, Leon, *The Life of Henry James,* published in four volumes: *The Untried Years* (Philadelphia, 1953), *The Conquest of London* (Philadelphia, 1962), *The Middle Years* (Philadelphia, 1962), *The Master* [in preparation]. Edel has compiled the definitive critical and biographical work on James' life and thought. *The Middle Years* deals with the period of *The Aspern Papers.*

James, Henry, *A Small Boy and Others* (New York, 1913), *Notes of a Son and Brother* (New York, 1914), *The Middle Years* (New York, 1917). These three volumes of James' autobiography are indispensable for an understanding of the author's conception of his life and art.

ASPERN PAPERS TEXT AND CRITICISM

Blackmur, Richard P. (ed.), *The Art of the Novel* (New York, 1947). These are James' critical prefaces to his stories and tales for the famed New York edition. The preface to *The Aspern Papers* written in 1908 details the origin of the story and elaborates on James' view of the "visitable past." In the preface James discusses the changes he made from the original facts of the Byron anecdote.

Bottkol, Joseph (ed.), *The Aspern Papers - The Europeans* (New York, 1950). The editor here has preserved the original English text of *The Aspern Papers* (published in 1888) and thus provides an interesting basis of comparison with the revised (1908) New York Edition generally available. In the introduction, Bottkol calls attention to an elaborate, if somewhat contrived, theory of Aspern as symbol for the god, Orpheus, and the critic as his initiate.

Edel, Leon (ed.), *Henry James Selected Fiction* (New York, 1953). In this collection, which includes *The Aspern Papers,* Edel follows each piece with the section of James' notebooks and the New York Edition preface which applies to it. He appends a brief, and always useful, comment to each piece.

Hoffman, Charles, *The Short Novels of Henry James* (New York, 1957). Hoffman divides James' short novels into the Early, Middle and Major periods. He discusses the works in terms of James' "period" themes. The book is carefully annotated and contains a detailed bibliography.

Matthiessen, F. O. and Murdock, Kenneth (ed.), *The Notebooks of Henry James* (New York, 1947). The crucial "gem" which provided the "facts" for *The Aspern Papers* is detailed by James in one of his surviving notebooks collected in this valuable edition.

GENERAL JAMES CRITICISM

Beach, Joseph Warren, *The Method of Henry James* (New Haven, 1918). An early but detailed and pathfinding analysis of the background and significance of James' style.

Dupee, F. W. (ed.), *The Question of Henry James* (New York, 1945). Dupee has collected a symposium of James criticism with selections from T. S. Eliot, Max Beerbohm and many others. Among the essays all the major points of James study are raised.

Matthiessen, F. O., *Henry James: The Major Phase* (New York, 1944). Looking at James' period of "great works" Matthiessen investigates the years 1895-1910 with great precision and insight.

Zabel, Morton D. (ed.), *The Indispensable Henry James* (New York, 1951). Although this collection does not include *The Aspern Papers*, it has a fine selection of letters, travel notes, criticism and tales. The introduction by Zabel contains a clear biography and a capsule account of James' artistic goals.

LETTERS

Edel, Leon, *Selected Letters of Henry James* (New York, 1960).

Lubbock, Percy, *The Letters of Henry James* (New York, 1920).

www.ingramcontent.com/pod-product-compliance
Lightning Source LLC
LaVergne TN
LVHW011735060526
838200LV00051B/3172